M000290448

Dear Uncle Hamp,
We hope you enjoy this
work from our baby girl.
love always
Donna & John   2020

|LIGHTS|
|CAMERA|
|ACTION|

A 40 DAY DEVOTIONAL TO HELP EXPOSE, EVOLVE, AND EXECUTE YOUR FAITH

DIAYLE J. DAVIS

I pray this
book blesses you
in a new way over
the next 40 days!
God Bless,
Diayle Davis

[handwritten inscription, illegible]

|LIGHTS|
|CAMERA|
|ACTION|

A 40 DAY DEVOTIONAL TO HELP EXPOSE, EVOLVE, AND EXECUTE YOUR FAITH

DIAYLE J. DAVIS

Halo
PUBLISHING
INTERNATIONAL

Lights| Camera| Action
A 40 day devotional to help expose, evolve, and execute your faith
Copyright © 2020 Diayle J. Davis
All rights reserved.

The Amplified Bible, Copyright 1954, 1958,1962, 1964, 1965,1987 by
The Lockman Foundation. Zondervan copyright 1987 by the Zondervan
Corporation and The Lockman Foundation. The following insert was
included on the copyright page of the Bible used, "Scripture quotations
taken from THE AMPLIFIED BIBLE, Copyright 1954, 1958,1962, 1964,
1965,1987 by The Lockman Foundation. All rights reserved. Used by
permission. (www.Lockman.org)".

No part of this book may be reproduced in any manner
whatsoever without the prior written permission of the publisher,
except in the case of brief quotations embodied in reviews.

ISBN: 978-1-61244-902-9
LCCN: 2020918470

Halo Publishing International, LLC
8000 W Interstate 10, Suite 600
San Antonio, Texas 78230
www.halopublishing.com

Printed and bound in the United States

I do not believe the term "thank you" is strong enough to express my gratitude to you for choosing this devotional. However, I have to extend a special thanks to my husband and children for their patience as I wrote. A thank you goes to my "test group" of readers, who provided feedback along the way. And lastly, I thank God for continuing to give me the words to say, for motivating me to continue when I wanted to quit, and for trusting me enough for this task.

In the following pages, you will find devotionals in which I share about times when I have been mad at God, others in which I share my personal struggles with fertility, and some in which I write about being challenged to the very core. Each day, for you and me both, will be different. Some days we will feel closer to God than the day before, and other days we will have to "force" ourselves to pray and read the Bible. On those days I hope you find something in this book to encourage your heart and mind.

Contents

Introduction

In this devotional, you will find Scriptures that have challenged my mindset as I have walked this journey with Christ, along with ways in which the Holy Spirit has prompted my heart to understand the Word better. I took many of these "promptings" from my journals, and then I added some elements (names are removed to "protect" the innocent) so that we may connect through these words. Over the two decades in which I have walked with Christ, I have transformed from a high school senior with no "faith foundation" to a woman—a public school teacher, a Christian counselor and coach, a wife, and a mother who tries DAILY to put God first in all aspects of life. I have experienced a range of emotions, periods of doubt, and areas of enlightenment. During those times, God has inspired my pen in order to encourage my heart, clarify times of confusion, and help me to understand His very nature on a deeper level. With that, this devotional is divided into three areas: **Lights, Camera,** and **Action.** The entries found in each area are meant to encourage you, challenge you to think about and connect with God's Word in a new way, and help you understand how the Word can be applied to your life so that you may grow deeper in your relationship with Him.

In my devotional time, I use an Amplified Bible, so you will find that the Scriptures from this translation accompany the devotionals. This translation includes additional translations of words and phrases using () and [], so this may cause passages to appear longer. However, I do not want you to feel "stuck" using this translation. I encourage you to explore each verse in whatever translation you prefer. Reading the Bible can be an overwhelming task, but I do not want you to put this book down because of this. For some days, I have included "notes" encouraging you to read more than just the verse(s) included. This is not "required," but it may give you more context and understanding.

I have included prayer "starters" with each devotional. These prayers follow the "A.C.T.S." prayer model: A = Adoration, C = Confession, T = Thanksgiving, and S = Supplication. These prayers can stand alone, or you can use them as a springboard as you communicate with God in your own way. Prayer is such an intimate conversation; you will find that I use various "names" to connect with our Heavenly Father. Sometimes I use the term "Daddy"—a very childlike term; one that many of us no longer use after a certain age—but I have found that this informal word reminds me that I should come to God with the faith of a child (Mt 18:2-4), fully relying on Him for my very life. Other times I may refer to Him as Jehovah, a name given to Him in the Old Testament. This is a term given to remind others of a particular characteristic of God. I may also use a term that Jesus Himself used: "Abba." This is the Aramaic term for "Father." Each of these terms display a personal connection to the Father, a way in which we can each connect to the God who intentionally chose to love each of us as a child. No matter what our natural, earthly family system looks like, we have a Heavenly Father who loves us more than we can fully comprehend, regardless of our faults and shortcomings. I have chosen to use a variety of terms, recognizing that each person who reads these pages may be at a different level of connection with God. But know that you should use whichever term works for you! Some days you might feel like "Yo, God" works, and other days you might just use a firm "Dad." I am certain the Father does not mind either one. He wants you to come to Him authentically, without pretense or false honor. He wants you to come as you are, baring all that you have at that moment.

My prayer as you enter the next forty days is that you learn something new about yourself, as well as something new about God. I hope that each day you will be challenged and convicted, but I also hope that you smile or laugh out loud along the way. I hope there is a statement that draws you one step closer to God, drawing you into a deeper relationship with Him. I pray you develop an urgency to put aside any areas that have caused you to stop believing, along with areas that have hardened your heart and dampened your spirit, so that you can feel a renewed sense of who God has fashioned you to be. I also pray that you find comfort in these pages, knowing that you are not alone in your journey. You are not alone. You are seen. You are His child. You are loved. You are forgiven. You are His hands and feet on this earth. You will experience highs and lows in life, but it will ALL work out for your good and His glory (Rom 8:28). You are incredible.

Heavenly Father, I thank You for Your continued love—a love that comforts me, reassures me, and builds me up. Thank You for the words in this book—words that have challenged me and will now challenge others. Your Word has convicted and corrected me, and I pray that this text does the same for the next person. Father, I pray for an open heart—one of repentance and a desire for change—because I know that there have been times in which I have sinned against You, believing that I knew better than You did, making choices that saddened Your heart. Thank You for Your forgiveness, for not turning Your back on me, instead walking me through this life patiently. I ask that You aid each person who picks up this book in the very area that he or she may need. I pray for confidence, comfort, understanding, correction, and conviction. Help each of us to receive something new with each day as we enter Your presence. Holy Spirit, draw us in and show us a new side of ourselves while revealing more of Your presence in our lives. Help our hearts and minds to be receptive to Your voice. May it be a comforting whisper on days when it's needed, and a loud shout on days when we seem to be hard of hearing. In Jesus' name, I pray. Amen.

Light(s)

A tool, when used correctly, essential to illuminating a dim/dark space and exposing what's hidden in the shadows. Light also provides aid when following directions, helps to reveal potential hazards on a journey, and expands sight beyond the darkness.

"Your word is a lamp to my feet and a light to my path" *(Ps 119:105 AMPC).*

You Are Chosen!

"You have not chosen Me, but I have chosen you and I have appointed you [I have planted you], that you might go and bear fruit and keep on bearing, and that your fruit may be lasting [that it may remain, abide], so that whatever you ask the Father in My Name [as presenting all that I AM], He may give it to you" (Jn 15:16 AMPC).

As I looked through old journals in preparation for the transparent journey that has been writing this devotional, I came across a prayer I'd written amid my fertility struggles. Just reading those words again caused the hurt, disappointment, and anguish to overwhelm me all over again. The opening line of that prayer was, "Am I broken?!?" I did not start with adoration or thanksgiving for how good God is; instead I just questioned whether the very awesome and unique person that is me, that God had created, was damaged and existing in error. I know I am not alone. Your struggle may not be with fertility; it may be with insecurity and rejection, figuring out your purpose, or deciding where to go next in life. Whatever it is, I want to reassure you, just as this passage has reassured me, that you are not broken. You are not out of place. You are not too old, too young, or too inexperienced. Above all else, you are loved, chosen because of who you are.

Jesus is talking to His disciples in this passage and the prior verse. He shifts their position from servants to friends, reminding them that they now have access to Him not as a distant employee, but as the inner circle. In the same way, God has selected each one of us to rest in the inner circle, a part of His "tribe." You and I have been handpicked and selected for a purpose, no matter what it looks like along the way. However, we have to seek God's wisdom and direction to understand what He desires for our lives. Even when we don't feel seen, valued, or important, God has created us for more. Sometimes we just don't see it.

I pray that you allow this to penetrate your heart and serve as a reminder in those moments that you feel less than enough. Remember that we did not choose to be loved by God or used by God; rather, He chose us just because. He didn't select us to "put us to work." Instead He wants to shower us with His love so that we may then shower others with the same love. That is the "work" that He desires of us: to make others feel seen, loved, and valuable. They are created for greatness, just as we are, by a Heavenly Father who has a love so deep for us.

Loving God, thank You for seeing me in those moments when I feel like I am not enough. Thank You for calling me into communion with You before I even knew I needed You. Holy Spirit, as I journey toward a deeper relationship with You, open my eyes, touch my spirit, and renew my mind so that I may see myself in You. I pray that Your Word will saturate my heart and mind so that I may see my areas of weakness and doubt, then develop in Your joy, peace, and power. In Jesus' name. Amen.

Constant Contact

"And Jesus, replying, said to them, Have faith in God [constantly]. Truly I tell you, whoever says to this mountain, Be lifted up and thrown into the sea! and does not doubt at all in his heart but believes that what he says will take place, it will be done for him. For this reason I am telling you, whatever you ask for in prayer, believe (trust and be confident) that it is granted to you, and you will [get it]. And whenever you stand praying, if you have anything against anyone, forgive him and let it drop (leave it, let it go), in order that your Father Who is in heaven may also forgive you your [own] failings and shortcomings and let them drop. But if you do not forgive, neither will your Father in heaven forgive your failings and shortcomings" (Mk 11:22-26 AMPC).

There was a period in my life when I was praying and fastvving often for the health of a friend. During one of those times, I read this Scripture and was challenged to shift my mindset. In the passage, I learned two things: I must be CONSTANT in my faith in God, and I must practice the art of forgiving myself.

Mark 11:22 states that I must have constant faith in God! That's all the time, regardless of which way my emotions swing, how my physical body feels, or if I'm in the mood to do the "whole Christian" (fully devoted follower) thing. We have to have faith, but just like everything else in our walks with Christ, it must be stretched and strengthened. We are in a spiritual battle, one that we have to be disciplined to fight in. Praying daily can be a challenge because life happens, but we should still take time to commune with the one who can make life a bit easier. Further, in the passage, the importance of forgiving others is emphasized, and I was reminded that I must also forgive myself. How could I truly have faith, truly repent, and truly deepen my intimacy with God if I did not fully forgive myself for my issues/sins/mistakes? If I was still harboring and dwelling on the things that I'd already gone to God about, I was putting myself in a position to be tempted by the enemy, tempted to doubt Christ's salvation, and tempted to question whether God had the ability/power/desire to do all that He promised.

From that moment forward, I thought about being nicer to myself and being more sensitive in my self-talk. I began to cut short anything that could challenge my belief in what God has said about me. I encourage you to think of these things as well. When was the last time you forgave yourself for a past mistake or a snarky comment made out of frustration or fatigue? When was the last time you looked in the mirror and complimented yourself? When was the last time you apologized to yourself for failing to stay committed to yourself (to your goals, your dreams, or your desires)?

Father, I praise You and adore You. I'm grateful for Your unconditional love and continuous grace—a grace that forgives even when I continue to make the same mistakes. Thank You for reminding me that Your arms are always open to comfort me and to wipe away the tears and pain I experience when I grow frustrated with myself. Holy Spirit, empower me today so that I may forgive myself, so that I may love myself a little deeper, and so that I may celebrate the person You have made me. I am because You have made me this way, helping me to grow more each day into the person You have called me to be for this season in life. In Jesus' name, I pray. Amen.

Facing the Cost of Self-Discipline

"I have told you these things, so that in Me you may have [perfect] peace and confidence. In the world you have tribulation and trials and distress and frustration; but be of good cheer [take courage; be confident, certain, undaunted]! For I have overcome the world. [I have deprived it of power to harm you and have conquered it for you.]" (Jn 16:33 AMPC).

"But [like a boxer] I buffet my body [handle it roughly, discipline it by hardships] and subdue it, for fear that after proclaiming to others the Gospel and things pertaining to it, I myself should become unfit [not stand the test, be unapproved and rejected as a counterfeit.]" (1 Cor 9:27 AMPC).

Before giving my life to Christ, I knew very little about the life of Christians, but I assumed that their lives were a lot easier. Boy, was I in for an awakening. I had the idea that everything in my life would be perfect, that I'd always be happy, that making future decisions would be easy, and that I would live in peace. Nevertheless, Jesus clearly warned us that we would have tribulations, that we would have to deal with worldly troubles. These things are all a part of the life that we must face when we lay down our selfish desires and follow Him. Even more, the Apostle Paul wrote that we would have to go through some rough "personal training." At times, being self-disciplined means laying down our sinful desires and doing the right thing by God's grace, no matter the cost. At other times, it means seeking God's direction. Seeking help to choose between "good" and "great."

"Dying to self" will bring necessary suffering—a suffering that is not always easy, similar to the lifestyle of a professional athlete. Choosing to be a top-performing athlete, in any sport, requires a person to follow a strict diet, extensive exercise regimens, and more. Each athlete makes this choice. Despite the feelings of fatigue, sore muscles, long hours, and missed life events, he or she still chooses the "suffering" to be better than the day before. This ideal is one that much of society applauds, as it's a commitment to one's craft. Likewise, we should consider our faith walk in the same way. To better resist temptation, we have to "die to self," or put aside what our bodies would naturally choose in order to do what God desires. In those moments, these choices may seem like suffering: choosing to abstain from food for a period of fasting in order to focus on prayer, logging off of social media to read the Bible more frequently, etc. You may miss things in those moments, therefore experiencing temporary suffering, but remember, even in the face of our suffering, there is hope! And as Paul stated, we can "Rejoice *and* exult in hope; be steadfast *and* patient in suffering and tribulation..." (Rom 12:12 AMPC). He also reminds us to be constant in prayer, seeking God's peace, joy, and wisdom, which will help us endure what is ahead of each of us.

Lord, You are my strength and support. You are my rock when I am unsure if I can continue to endure the troubles I face, and for that, I am so thankful. Your word renews my heart and mind and refills my sense of hope. So I am making the decision, in advance, to please You, whether my flesh is willing or not. Even if I need to suffer to do Your will, I know that there is hope, for Your Spirit is in me, and You have overcome the world and will aid me as I overcome temptation, doubt, fear, and so much more as I live this life. Holy Spirit, help me to endure with joy, peace, and patience, even when the pressure seems too great. In the name of Jesus. Amen.

Desiring God More Than His Blessings

"Let your character or moral disposition be free from love of money [including greed, avarice, lust, and craving for earthly possessions] and be satisfied with your present [circumstances and with what you have]; for He [God] Himself has said, I will not in any way fail you nor give you up nor leave you without support. [I will] not, [I will] not, [I will] not in any degree leave you helpless nor forsake nor let [you] down (relax My hold on you)! [Assuredly not!]" (Heb 13:5 AMPC).

I'm sure that many of us have that "one thing"—maybe more than one thing—that we believe we cannot live without. In high school, my "thing" was a particular brand of jeans that my parents refused to buy because of the price tag. In college, that "thing" was to find the guy who would be my husband after graduation. Once I got married (and not to the guy I dated in college), my "thing" was to become a mother, only to find that I would endure fertility issues. Throughout each of these times, I looked to tangible things as ways to define myself, then dealt with feelings such as jealousy, disappointment, and rejection when I could not obtain them. I tried to ignore those feelings, seeing them as being ungodly. But honestly, how many of us can say, "I am not jealous of anyone else or envious of what others have. If God gave it to them, then I want them to enjoy it," each time someone else gets what we want before we do.

Hebrews 13:5 challenges us on this very thing. "Let your conduct be without covetousness; be content with such things as you have" (Heb 13:5 NKJV). I believe God tests us to see if we will live by this verse. There are times when He will put somebody in front of us who has exactly what we want, just to see how we will respond. Will we celebrate and worship God alongside them, or will our hearts harden with jealousy and resentment? Will we surrender the hurt and disappointment of not receiving what we want to the God who wants to handle all those feelings with us? Until we can pass His "I am happy for you because you are blessed" test, we are never going to have any more than what we have right now.

If you have asked God for something and He has not given it to you yet, do not lose heart. He is not holding out on you to cause hurt; He simply wants to make sure He remains the Lord of your life and that this "thing" has not become an idol above Him. God desires for us to prosper in every way. He wants the entire world to see how good He is and how well He takes care of His children. However, we must desire God more than we desire His blessings.

Daddy, I want You to reveal the areas in my life where I have given in to jealousy and covetousness. Help me to rearrange my priorities, keeping You first and being grateful for the areas of my life that You have already decided to bless. I want to desire You above all that You can give me. Thank You for all that You have given me in this life. Thank You for the things to come and the things that will not, because both are done in love. Amen.

The Devil's in the Details

"Let them make Me a sanctuary, that I may dwell among them. [Heb.8:1,2;10:1] And you shall make it according to all that I show you, the pattern of the tabernacle or dwelling and the pattern of all the furniture of it" (Ex 25:8-9 AMPC).

In Exodus 24-31, God provides Moses with a very detailed plan for the tabernacle. As I read the encounter between God and Moses, I marveled at the amount of detail that God invested in this plan in order to create a place for Himself to embody, a place to speak with His children. It made me think of how detailed His plan must be for my life. I can only imagine the measurements and outlines that He has spread out throughout my life.

The amount of detail also overwhelmed me. As a reader, it seemed like overkill to a certain degree. I started to get anxious just reading it, and had flashbacks to trying to build furniture from IKEA. So many pictures...so few words... so many extra, leftover pieces...nightmares! Did God really need to be so meticulous? I started to think of how overwhelming this encounter had to be for Moses. What if he got a measurement wrong, or what if he skipped a step entirely? Would God's presence be able to enter as He intended? Again, I thought of God's purpose for me. I'm sure my plan is also very detailed, and if delivered all at once, it would be quite overwhelming, so I'm grateful to receive it in portions.

Unfortunately, the book of Exodus does not end there. In chapter 32, the people of Israel threw all the hard work of Moses out of the window. They felt that lives of blessings, holiness, and virtue took too long to explain. After years of slavery, with God revealing His love and affection for them, they simply said, "Forget Moses. He's taking too long, and we don't even know if he's coming back." This stood out to me, forcing me to ask some hard questions. How often have I delayed the start of my journey into the "Promise Land" because the start of the trip was taking too long? What have I created as a Golden Calf (an artificial idol) in my life because I haven't let God's blueprint take shape?

After reading this story, this old saying came to mind: "The devil is in the details." In this situation, it may be true. In this passage, God gave so many details that more time passed than the people of Israel cared to wait, allowing time for them to succumb to their own selfish and sinful nature. The passage of time has healing effects, but it also opens the doorway for our evil nature to take control. We have to remember that there is a plan, and for that plan to be a success, we have to wait for the details.

Daddy, I thank You for planning my life before the very beginning of time. For keeping in mind everything that I need to accomplish and the tasks You've destined for me to complete during my time on Earth. Help me to not be overwhelmed by the details in the plan or the delays that will come along the way. At the end of the day, Your plan—with all the details, delays, and detours—will help me to reach an outstanding destination. I praise You for thinking enough of me to execute the journey along with You. In Jesus' name. Amen.

What's Your Why?

"For ever since the creation of the world His invisible nature and attributes, that is, His eternal power and divinity, have been made intelligible and clearly discernible in and through the things that have been made (His handiworks). So [men] are without excuse [altogether without any defense or justification], Because when they knew and recognized Him as God, they did not honor and glorify Him as God or give Him thanks. But instead they became futile and godless in their thinking [with vain imaginings, foolish reasoning, and stupid speculations] and their senseless minds were darkened" (Rom 1:20-21 AMPC).

There was a time when I would share my thoughts about a particular Scripture with friends through e-mail or on a blog, much as I am sharing with you now. However, there were times when I shared not for God to be glorified, but for the positive feedback and comments. So when those things didn't come, I felt rejected. That rejection caused me to put more pressure on myself. I was expecting so much out of my time with God that I lost sight of the true intention. These verses help me to move out of the way, reminding me that God wants to and will always work in His handiwork, but oftentimes we choose not to see it. We, as His children, should be able to discern His presence, but when we choose to over-analyze His behavior, overthink, and have more "faith" in our abilities, we fail!

Even more, these verses made me think about this: "What am I doing to recognize God's power and hand on me, around me, and working through me?" I came up with

NOTHING! Nevertheless, that only made me think more. We don't recognize His presence all around us, and then we question why we still struggle with certain sins. We're getting in our own way. Are we behaving like the Romans, who chose to analyze God's behavior rather than glorifying His handiwork? Are we taking pride in our actions by gloating and patting ourselves on the back? We fall into this trap all the time! We think we "run" things, and we're just as foolish as they were. When we make ourselves the center, we have done nothing but turn the glory away from the one who rightly deserves the applause, accolades (the degrees, promotions, etc.), and attention.

Abba Father, thank You for being patient with me, for reminding me of Your love and willingness to wait around for me to come to my senses. I am sorry for the many times that I have placed the recognition of others, the "likes" on social media, and the praise of strangers above being genuine in my time spent with You. Today, I ask that You open my eyes to see the areas in which I have more confidence in myself than I do in Your handiwork. Holy Spirit, help me to step down from the throne that I have placed myself on. Help me to allow the Lord of all the earth to take His rightful place. In Jesus' name. Amen.

Bringing them Out of Darkness!

"The people who sat (dwelt enveloped) in darkness have seen a great Light, and for those who sat in the land and shadow of death Light has dawned. From that time Jesus began to preach, crying out, Repent (change your mind for the better, heartily amend your ways, with abhorrence of your past sins), for the kingdom of heaven is at hand" Mt 4:16-17 AMPC).

During a sermon series, my pastor challenged me to understand my assignment as an ambassador of Christ. I was challenged to recognize that through my salvation I was not just given eternal life; I was also given a ministry and a purpose to fulfill. Now, you may read this and think, "And? We have all been given a purpose. I've even spent forty days reading that book to figure mine out, so what's your point?" Well, my point is that our purpose, our ministry, is far simpler than we would have it to be. The text says that there was a group of people "enveloped in darkness" who were shown a great light after Christ began to teach. When was the last time you can say you exposed someone to the Light of Christ? Better yet, when was the last time you were so engulfed and saturated by the Light of Christ that you seemed to radiate with His presence, and strangers on the street simply had to ask what is going on in your life?

II Corinthians 5:17-21 simply explains our ministry and purpose to us. That text teaches us that our ministry and purpose are the same. We are created not only to worship the Father but also to bring others to Him. How are you doing in that area? Are you allowing your Light to shine before men (Mt 5:16)? Are you committing yourself to the Father so that you may be used by Him to bring others into His kingdom? Or are you simply holding your salvation to yourself, content knowing that you have eternal life and that is all that matters?

However, is that all that matters? I don't know about you, but I would love to hear my Heavenly Father say to me as I stand before Him, "Good Job, baby girl. I'm proud of you." If you have never heard those words from a natural parent, it may be difficult to imagine. Nevertheless, think about how joyous it will be to hear it from the Father who sought you out, who loved you more than life, as He committed a part of Himself to die for you. Open your heart to be sensitive to His voice. Take time out to rest in His presence, growing in His word, acknowledging daily all that He's done so that you may be a vessel used by Him. Accept your ministry and begin walking in your purpose. Your job is to help bring the lost back to their Creator. Will you help, or will you hinder?

Abba, Father, You are our Savior and Lord. You are truly a blessing in my life. I cannot fully imagine who or where I would be without Your love, grace, and mercy. I humbly come before You, asking Your forgiveness. Forgiveness from sin, forgiveness from apathy, and forgiveness from being lukewarm in my desire to hunt after You. On this day, begin to change my heart so that I may have a new thirst for you. Daddy, give me a clear understanding of my position and assignment in You. Yes, You have given me gifts and talents. Yes, I may serve in ministries at my local church, but if all I do fails to benefit the unsaved, the backsliders, or even the believers, show me how I need to be better used. In Jesus' name, I humbly lay my life down before You, accepting the call to be an ambassador for Your Kingdom. Amen.

Steadfast! Unwavering! Unmovable!

"For I desire and delight in dutiful steadfast love and good-ness, not sacrifice, and the knowledge of and acquaintance with God more than burnt offerings" (Hos 6:6 AMPC).

During college, I joined a Christian sorority, which placed me *and* my faith front and center among my peers. Unfortunately, during that time, I also dealt with a season in which I was mad at God, but I could not publically share that since it would conflict with the image that I needed to maintain as a part of the ministry. This verse reminded me that God desires more than just a show from you and me. Your relationship with Christ is not about the fact that you have spent all day fasting, praying, singing in the choir, etc. If your heart's not in what He's called you to do, you might as well stop. Your fast becomes a diet, your worship a chore, and your service a pain. When this happens, you, my friend, become lukewarm in your relationship with the Father.

Your life should be a reflection of your relationship with God. If you are constantly complaining about the things you do for the Kingdom of God, then step back and do a spot check. First, ask yourself if God desires for you to do those activities. Second, check with God about the state/condition of your heart. Have you hardened your heart toward a situation or group of people because you do not necessarily agree with, or even fully understand, the plan that God has for those people. Well, Jonah, you have no say in what God wants to do on His earth, with His people, as His vessel. So, get a heart exam and make sure you aren't serving the Lord with bitterness, frustration, malice, contempt, or laziness. Finally, ask for a rekindling of the passion you had as a new convert. Return to the time when the only thing that mattered was pleasing God, studying the Word of God, and sharing the goodness and mercy of God. Now you barely say grace or "God bless you" after someone sneezes.

Please, friend, do not lose sight of the one who orchestrated every element of this life so that you may be where you are today. He simply wants your love in return. He desires to bestow upon you a life you could never imagine, but He wants to love on you first, so love Him in return. Love Him not out of obligation, but out of reverence, out of adoration, and out of want for who He has been to you. Once you focus on His love, you will not mind laboring for His Kingdom, as it is truly the least we can do after all He has done for us.

Lord, I magnify Your name. I glorify Your name, for You are good, and Your mercy endures forever. Your love never fails. Despite all that I do and think, You constantly remind me that You love me. The gentle breezes in the summer, the close parking space in the winter, and the warm embrace of a friend when things are difficult are all ways that You shower me with love. The most important display was becoming sin for me. I will not have to endure the unending torture of hell because I failed to return to a loving relationship with You. Show me ways that I can love You more. Take me out of my comfort zone and push me to the limit so that I can only see You as my source. Help me to hear Your call, seek Your face, and wait for the right time to move. Teach me to love You on a deeper level so that I may be sensitive to Your voice. Teach me to love myself so that I may see the value in my life and the worth that You see, so that I don't continue to resort to temporary pleasures that come with sin in order to find value in life. I ask all these things in Jesus' name, giving thanks in advance for the journey You're going to take me on. Amen.

Taking an Inside Look

"Jesus answered, It was not that this man or his parents sinned, but he was born blind in order that the workings of God should be manifested (displayed and illustrated) in him" (Jn 9:3 AMPC).

Each year, as I near my birthday, I often become very reflective, especially in recent years, as I approach a new decade (runs to hide). I'm sure I'm not alone. It may not be near your birthday. It may be as the calendar nears a significant date, like the loss of a loved one or an anniversary, or as another year begins. But we all go through periods of self-reflection and introspection. During those periods of reflection, I wrestled with a few questions. How has God's power been seen in my life? What areas—which I assumed were part of my core personality—have I allowed God to come in and change?

This passage helped to answer those questions for me. Well, they at least pointed me in the right direction so I could start to uncover the answers. Jesus is addressing a physical ailment in this passage, but we may have an emotional ailment to be healed. We each have personality "quirks"—an attitude problem, a flirtatious personality, or a quick temper. But are those qualities and characteristics of God? No? Then how can we say that God made us this way. I doubt He did. It's these areas, and others like it, that God wants to change or remove from our lives so that His power, His authority, and His love can show through each of us.

I was also reminded to avoid shortchanging God or blocking my blessings because I failed to allow God to come in and change things for His glory. He desires to make you and me complete, molding us into His image (inside and out), but He requires it ALL. We have to hold back nothing, intentionally taking everything to Him and leaving it before Him so that His power may be displayed and others may see His Light radiating from us.

Abba Father, I bless Your name. I exalt You above all. I thank You for Your desire to complete me. Thank You for surrounding me with Your love and power. You fill me with your presence, and I am so grateful. Holy Spirit, help me to uncover those areas that You desire to change for my good and Your glory. Help me mature in You so others may be able to see You in me. In Jesus' name, I pray. Amen.

Give Honor

"Therefore, O king, let my counsel be acceptable to you; break off your sins and show the reality of your repentance by righteousness (right standing with God and moral and spiritual rectitude and rightness in every area and relation) and liberate yourself from your iniquities by showing mercy and loving-kindness to the poor and oppressed, that [if the king will repent] there may possibly be a continuance and lengthening of your peace and tranquility and healing of your error" (Dn 4:27 AMPC).

Read the chapter in its entirety

Throughout my academic career (high school through graduate school), I was always a strong student. I'm talking top five percent of my class and multiple semesters with a 4.0 GPA. My habit of procrastinating was often followed by stellar grades, and last-minute cramming brought near-perfect test scores. Those habits resulted in a sense of pride in my abilities. This pride was not the type of pride that a parent feels when their child proves that hard work and dedication can result in a full scholarship for college, but I had hubris in my own skills.

Unfortunately, that hubris eventually led to disappointment and frustration. I assumed that my skills would always bring positive outcomes. I saw myself as being a "gift" to others because of my abilities, until God reminded me otherwise. In the fourth chapter of Daniel, we see the very same thing happening. King Nebuchadnezzar thought so highly of himself that God was forced to humble him to the point of humiliation. I am happy to say that God never humbled me in the same way as this king, but I had to learn the reality that I am nothing unless I submit and walk under the authority of God. I learned that I could not be prideful or conceited, especially when I only accomplished things because God gave me those opportunities.

You and I must remember that He can humble each of us, reducing us to nothing so that His name may be glorified. This is not to reduce or diminish our status as His children, but to remind us that we can place ourselves on the "throne" of our hearts, moving God from His position as Lord to the second in command. Neither you nor I are in control of our lives. It is not for us to dictate the things of the Father, nor should we believe that we have accomplished anything in our power and strength. Recognizing that He is God and that He should be our safe dwelling place—not someone we can place on our level, as we are nowhere close to His level—is important in fighting against the pride we may begin to feel in our abilities.

Father, You have chosen to love me, flaws and all. Help me to remember that You have gifted me with certain talents and abilities to be used for Your glory. Each gift I have allows me to influence the world around me so that others may know Your love, Your mercy and grace, and Your compassion. Many times I can get in the way, thinking too highly of myself rather than humbly appreciating that You have designed me for such a time as this. Thank You for loving me enough to give me gifts and talents to be used for the good of others. Help me to steward those gifts in a way that glorifies Your name. In Jesus' name. Amen.

Laundry Day

"Blessed (happy and to be envied) are those who cleanse their garments, that they may have the authority and right to [approach] the tree of life and to enter through the gates into the city" (Rv 22:14 AMPC).

"For by a single offering He has forever completely cleansed and perfected those who are consecrated and made holy" (Heb 10:14 AMPC).

Since moving out on my own and taking on the full responsibility of the "chores" in my home, I have developed a love/hate relationship with laundry. There was once a time when laundry was fun, which was when I was only responsible for throwing clothes into the washing machine or for finding matching socks. However, when it was my turn to sort the clothes, remember to move the clothes from the washing machine to the dryer, and then (the part that I think might be the worst) fold and put those clothes away, this task truly became a chore. I hope I am not the only one who feels this way. I hate the process, but I love the feeling of clothes right out of the dryer. And I love being able to put on a favorite shirt or pair of jeans without having to look for it.

Clean clothes are evidence that a process has been completed; stains are removed, and a fresh fragrance remains. These passages should remind us that we, too, go through a cleaning process. We are stained from our sins, but if we pursue righteousness and seek holiness, we experience a cleansing. We are made holy in Him, but we must continue to turn away from our sins. His love and perfection stir up something new within us: a desire to be washed anew, removing the stains in the process. Also, this cleansing effect helps us to clear away the clutter, helping us to hear from Him and giving us access to the Father, but the first step is to accept Christ into our hearts. He is the pre-wash, the step that loosens those "set-in stains," or those sins that make up just "who we are." However, God does not leave us there; the Holy Spirit comes to penetrate and activate the deep cleaning process, sanctifying each of us into God's image.

But we must ask ourselves: Where are we in the process? Have you sorted out the areas of your life that require a delicate cycle, separating those areas that only require a gentle washing (small adjustments in behavior and mindset) from those that require a deep, heavy-duty cleaning (areas that may only come clean through prayer and fasting, and for some areas a Christian counselor)? As much as we may want to, we can't put off this chore forever, either in our homes or in our hearts. Eventually, the stains will become too apparent, and someone will notice.

Jehovah Mephalti, the Lord My Deliverer, thank You for Your cleansing love and grace. Thank You for loving me enough to not leave me in a place separated from You. Father, please forgive me for the times that I have sinned against You, times that I chose poorly. I am grateful that Your presence continues to cleanse me, wiping away the parts of me that are unlike You. Holy Spirit, as I continue this life, give me the courage to endure the cleansing process, the deep cleaning of my thoughts, feelings, and actions. Even though it may be challenging, it will be beneficial, and I trust Your wisdom above my own. In Jesus' name, I pray. Amen.

Crushed

"When my soul fainted upon me [crushing me], I earnestly and seriously remembered the Lord; and my prayer came to You, into Your Holy temple" (Jon 2:7 AMPC).

A few times, I have felt crushed by the events in my life. It seemed like everything was happening at the same time. One time in particular was in the summer after I graduated from college. I was in the process of looking for a job as a teacher and redecorating my childhood room into something more "adult." While standing in a home improvement store, I received a phone call I would never forget. A mutual friend was calling to tell me that our friend was on life support, and simply asked that I pray. As you can imagine, I cried in that very spot. This was a friend whom I had spoken with the week before as she traveled for work, and we agreed to a lunch date after I returned from a trip of my own. We never had that lunch date. Within a span of ten days, a strong, vibrant young woman was dead at twenty-one. At the same time, I was interviewing for jobs and was denied in two different districts. As you can imagine, I was experiencing a range of negative emotions: rejection, grief, and confusion. I was left questioning God about so many things. Why did He allow my friend, who was the only child of a single mother, to die? Why did He call me to a career, then close doors in my face? Why did this loss hurt so bad?

Throughout this time, I was numb. I could barely pray. I was living on autopilot. I wasn't taking the time to ask for God's direction. I was only existing. I didn't pray before interviews. I just knew that the school year was about to start, and I was unemployed. But despite how I felt, God knew what I needed, and He brought me to this passage, specifically Jonah 2:5-9. His Word reminded me that when all else fails, when you can't do it on your own, and when your physical strength has failed and you get tired of walking under your authority, you'll turn to Christ. Although this passage was reassuring, letting me know that God will hear our prayers when we are at the very end of our rope, it also challenged me not to wait until I was completely depleted to turn to Him. If your life is truly in the hands of the Father, you shouldn't try to do things on your own. You should position yourself in a way that will allow God to be both Savior and Lord.

Have you been in similar seasons in life? Times in which everything seems to be closing in on you? In my case, it was the devastating loss of a friend combined with the frustration of searching for a job. For you, it may be strained familial relationships causing a rift between loved ones. Or the stressors of financial hardships causing debt to grow, with no end in sight. Or overwhelming pressures at work causing physical damage to your body. Whatever "it" is for you, remember that you are not alone. The God of heaven and Earth wants to lift you up and is ready to listen when you cry out to Him.

Jehovah El Roi, the Lord who sees, You are ever faithful in meeting my needs, from the smallest to the largest. You watch over me in my valleys and at my peaks, and I am so grateful for Your covering. Help me to be sensitive to Your prompting so that I may not lose sight of Your guidance and direction. Father, I pray for a renewed passion for Your Word so that I may seek Your face daily, not only in prayer, but also in study. Give me an unquenchable thirst for Your teachings. In Jesus' name. Amen.

Return to Your First Love

"And she shall follow after her lovers but she shall not overtake them; and she shall seek them [inquiring for and requiring them], but shall not find them. Then shall she say, Let me go and return to my first husband, for then was it better with me than now. For she has not noticed, understood, or realized that it was I [the Lord God] Who gave her the grain and the new wine and the fresh oil, and Who lavished upon her silver and gold which they used for Baal and made into his image" (Hos 2:7-8 AMPC).

In this passage, God likens the children of Israel to a prostitute woman—a woman who chases after "lovers," believing that her lovers have given her numerous material goods, failing to understand that God has given her everything she needs. She makes matters worse by dedicating the things that God has given her to Baal, a god of the surrounding nations. We do the same thing. We may not worship another god, but we may put our jobs in place of our true relationship with the Father. We may even place our friends and family above the Father. I know there have been times when I have done that very thing. Early in my marriage, I expected my husband to fill a void that rightfully belonged to God, but that error in expectation only led to frustration, both with God and my husband. However, once I dug into these verses, I was reminded that my marriage was a very good gift from God.

I encourage you to examine your life and your heart. Are you putting things before God? Are you taking the honor due to God for yourself, failing to acknowledge His handiwork in your life? Are you failing to give God what He deserves, such as your time, talent, and treasures? Recognize your actions, and soon you will recognize that you are not always loving God as you think. Show Him the love and appreciation that He rightly deserves, because if you don't, He will begin to remove things, saying "no" to things so you will remember who He is and what His rightful place is in your life. But remember, you cannot try to play God. He knows that if your life doesn't turn out how you want it, you'll run to Him. You cannot turn God into a genie or treat Him like a vending machine. He is a jealous God (Jo 24:19), not an afterthought.

It may take time to uncover these areas in your life, and it may take even longer to vocalize and acknowledge God for all He has done for you. In our culture, we have been taught over and over that when we succeed, we've done so individually, having done all the work for our success, and we should take the credit for it. Unfortunately, that's often not the case. In our professions, there are others who help mentor us and build us up. In our communities, there are people who work behind the scenes to get things accomplished for the whole community, often with no recognition. Likewise, we treat God the same way, failing to recognize the one who loved each of us before the Earth was formed, the one who has showered us with gifts unimaginable. He simply desires for us to acknowledge His presence in our lives.

Jehovah Shammah (The Lord Is There). Your Word tells me repeatedly that You are always with me. Unfortunately, I forget and place other things above You. Forgive me for that, for choosing other lovers above You. Holy Spirit, help me to return to You, my first love. You loved me before life began, creating me for a reason. Even when I have turned my back on You, You continue to give me what I need, even when I don't deserve it. Thank You for Your faithfulness and love beyond measure. Help me to remember that You are my first love and that You desire the best for me. Holy Spirit, continue to guide me back to You when I step off the path You've designed for me. In Jesus' name. Amen.

Shine Bright

"And the light shines on in the darkness, for the darkness has never overpowered it [put it out or absorbed it or appropriated it, and is unreceptive to it]" (Jn 1:5 AMPC).

Throughout my teaching career, I did not allow students to use profanity in my classroom, expressing that I typically only heard it in movies and occasionally in music. I was not opposed to it for a faith-based reason, although Ephesians 4:29 is hidden in my heart for this very reason, but if I hear it too frequently, the old habit of "coloring" my speech with it could return. I did not come to Christ until my senior year of high school, so certain behaviors were my normal, like using profanity and pre-marital sex. But this verse serves as a frequent reminder that no matter what I'm exposed to, the Light within me is still greater.

Despite what you think, your light will always shine. Despite how much you try and put it out, your relationship with the Father, your knowledge of His Son, and the indwelling of His Spirit guarantee that you will walk as a child of the Light. For that Light will always expose the dark areas that we try to shield from the Holy Spirit as He tries to convict and correct. But you can do things to cause your Light to dim. You stop having devotional time. You stop spending time in prayer. You only attend church on major holidays, or even worse, you begin to view your relationship with the Creator of the world, the God who gives life to EVERY living thing, as an obligation, never seeking to truly know Him. This can dim your Light as you grow insensitive to His power, to His love, and His voice. Thankfully, the Light of Christ will continue to shine no matter what you have around you, allowing each of us to rekindle the flame that lives within.

Light of the World, thank You for Your consistent presence in my life. You continue to remind me that You are always there, even during times when I try to run and hide. Thank You for reminding me through Your Word that Your Light overpowers those dark moments when I try to live a life that is opposite of what You have said I should live. Forgive me for those times when I allowed my environment to dim my Light. Forgive me for the times when I thought I was strong enough to resist past temptations, only to allow them to extinguish my Light instead.

Camera

A tool, when used correctly, that is important for the capturing of an image, still or animated. Its purpose is to produce a replica of the image that it captures. The camera must endure a process of development for the reproduction of the image to be completed.

"Every Scripture is God-breathed (given by His inspiration) and profitable for instruction, for reproof and conviction of sin, for correction of error and discipline in obedience, [and] for training in righteousness (in holy living, in conformity to God's will in thought, purpose, and action), So that the man of God may be complete and proficient, well fitted and thoroughly equipped for every good work" (2 Tm 3:16-17 AMPC).

Called to Consistency

"Keep the charge of the Lord your God, walk in His ways, keep His statutes, His Commandments, His precepts, and His testimonies..." (1 Kgs 2:3 AMPC).

"But as the One Who called you is holy, you yourselves also be holy in all your conduct and manner of living. For it is written, You shall be, for I am holy" (1 Pt 1:15-16 AMPC).

During a time early in my faith, I was still in the process of figuring out the personality of God for myself. Before committing my life to Christ, I did not have much knowledge of the personality or character of God beyond what I'd heard in the few church services I'd attended as a child. I spent time trying to learn Him more, to get a better understanding of this God who loves me unconditionally and who was concerned about my life before I was even born. As years passed, I began to make connections between the God of the Old Testament and the teaching in the New Testament. One attribute I found is that He is consistent and expects us to be consistent in our walks with Him, as well. These two passages are wonderful examples of that. The charge that is given in I Kings 2:3 is reinforced by Peter, who reminds us to live a life of holiness because God is holy. We are to walk in His ways. We are to follow His statues, or directions, so that we may grow in and experience the holiness of God.

With these two verses in mind, the Holy Spirit pushed me to be reflective, asking challenging questions in light of my relationship with God. Have I been doing what needs to be done so that I am true in worship? Has my behavior been pleasing in the sight of the Lord, not just a mask for those around me "watching"? What can I do to change for the better in all areas of my life, not just in my faith? Just as I was challenged, I would like to challenge you to think about those things. Are you living a life of holiness in a way that allows you to "keep the charge of the Lord your God"?

Daddy, I praise You for Your gentle reminders, for Your loving correction, and for simply being a consistent presence in my life. You are so worthy of adoration and thanks. There are often times when I have relied on old habits to get through life—habits that are not pleasing to You—and I ask that You forgive me for the wrong choices I have made. I thank You for reaffirming that I need to rest in You above all things, for You are the source of my strength, and You can only be glorified through me if I am sincerely serving You. Daddy, help me. Create in me a clean heart so that I might serve You. Show me the areas in which I need to change so You may be exalted above the highest.

New Seasons

"Now, O Lord my God, You have made Your servant king instead of David my father, and I am but a lad [in wisdom and experience]; I know not how to go out (begin) or come in (finish). Your servant is in the midst of Your people whom You have chosen, a great people who cannot be counted for multitude. So give Your servant an understanding mind and a hearing heart to judge Your people, that I may discern between good and bad. For who is able to judge and rule this Your great people?" (1 Kgs 3:7-9 AMPC).

Can I tell you something? The change of seasons is my favorite way to watch God's miraculous works. Watching God create the coloring book that many of us call autumn, the sweet smell of spring as flowers bloom, and the crisp, clean look of winter…it amazes me each year. It's as if it were brand new. Beyond the natural change of seasons, we each experience our own change of seasons, and with each change, we need something different. There are many times in those new seasons when we find ourselves unprepared (failing to have the necessary skills and/or resources for success) or underprepared (lacking the adequate training or resources needed for success). I found myself in that place when, after two years of trying to conceive, my husband and I gave birth to our daughter. Seventeen months after my daughter was born, my son was born without need for treatments, expanding my "kingdom" as a stay-at-home mom, a season in my life that was so very new. Since that time, I have prayed earnestly for God to give me the wisdom to "rule over my people."

I needed God's divine wisdom to parent them effectively. I was intentional in building relationships with each one so that as they grew, we did not enter into power struggles. And by power struggles, I mean potty training. Moreover, I also wanted to have the ability to model God's love, mercy, and grace for each of them, which meant I required God's wisdom and grace along the way. Some days it was hard. I felt both unprepared and underprepared, but I found comfort in knowing that God had given me a gift and would give me the grace to navigate this season of change.

In every season of change, I encourage you to ask yourself these questions: Are you ready for the change to come? Are you ready for your life as a leader (as a spouse, as a parent, etc.), even if you feel unprepared? Have you positioned yourself to walk in obedience in this new season? Have you been intentional in seeking the wisdom and guidance of your Heavenly Father as you transition from one season to the next? Each question will result in a different answer depending on the season, so continue to ask yourself these hard questions and still yourself to hear the answers.

Heavenly Father, thank You. Thank You for always being available. Even when I do not feel close to You, Your Spirit is with me, Your love covers and protects me, and for that I am so grateful. Your Word tells me that if I need wisdom, seek it out. Solomon walked in Your wisdom, and You were glorified. I, too, desire to walk in Your wisdom so that I may be an example of Your godly guidance and direction. Fill me with Your Spirit so that I may glorify Your name above the heavens. Help me to seek after Your will with all my being so that I may be graced for this change to come. Father, in times when I feel less than because I do not feel prepared, reassure me of Your presence. In Jesus' name, I pray. Amen.

A Gift is Given, Not Earned

"He saved us, not because of any works of righteousness that we had done, but because of His own pity and mercy, by [the] cleansing [bath] of the new birth (regeneration) and renewing of the Holy Spirit, Which He poured out [so] richly upon us through Jesus Christ our Savior. [And He did it in order] that we might be justified by His grace (by His favor, wholly undeserved), [that we might be acknowledged and counted as conformed to the divine will in purpose, thought, and action], and that we might become heirs of eternal life according to [our] hope" (Ti 3:5-7 AMPC).

Every child seems to be more conscious of his behavior around gift-giving occasions: birthdays, holidays, and report card time. However, the greatest gift that has been given to the world was given to us when Christ laid down His life so that we might return to a relationship with the Father. It is important that we remember that there was nothing we could have done to earn that gift from God. God, the Father, planned to give the world His Son so that we may be redeemed, *not* because we earned it, but because He desired reconciliation and restoration between Himself and His creation. If it were not for the mercy of God, there would be no option for salvation. There is no amount of volunteer work, money, or church services that will earn your entrance into heaven. It is when the Father calls you, and you earnestly answer, that you will enter.

We each need to accept that this gift, the gift of salvation, has been given because of God's grace, love, mercy, and deep desire to be in communion with each of us. And it is just that: a gift. Not to be earned, but to simply be received with an open heart. I encourage you to accept this gift, acknowledging the giver with a "thank you." Do not simply say thank you with your mouth during worship or your mind during prayer, but also give thanks in your actions through your pursuit of righteousness. Show your appreciation by loving your neighbor as yourself (Mt 22:39). Show your gratitude in your professional life and in your service of others.

Gracious God, I thank You for this unbelievable gift that You have given me. I so appreciate Your love, which was a love that I did not know I needed until after I received it. There have been times when I have taken advantage of the gift You've given me, neglecting the opportunities that You've opened for me, and for that I am sorry. Yet You love me nonetheless. Help me to share that love with others. Help me to live a life of appreciation and worship for You. As I continue to love on You, help me to love myself and others in the same way, extending grace and mercy as You have shown it to me. In Jesus' name, I pray. Amen.

Don't Be Afraid!

"And you, son of man, be not afraid of them, neither be afraid of their words; though briers and thorns are all around you and you dwell and sit among scorpions, be not afraid of their words nor be dismayed at their looks, for they are a rebellious house. And you shall speak My words to them whether they will hear or refuse to hear, for they are most rebellious. As for you, son of man, hear what I say to you; be not rebellious like that rebellious house; open your mouth and eat what I give you" (Ez 2:6-8 AMPC).

During college, I, along with some friends, partnered with a local ministry to share the Gospel in a local neighborhood. We were divided into teams. One team went door to door, and the other stayed behind to pray. After that experience, I was certain that "street evangelism" wasn't for me. Walking up to strangers and sharing the love of God didn't mesh with my personality. But I know that God has given us a great love, so we must share it. We must be willing to go to places we do not feel comfortable so we can share the Word of God. Ezekiel is given the task of going to speak with Israel. Who have you been given the task to speak to? The text shows us that God wants Ezekiel to move without fear of what people are going to say. He knew that people would reject him. He knew that people would bad-mouth him. But He charged him to go anyway, and to go without fear. We should not be ashamed; we should not stop sharing the love God graciously gave because we are afraid of how someone will respond.

Nevertheless, in verse eight, we learn that we will be fully equipped to handle the scorpions, thorns, and briers. Or let's make it real: the drug-addicted family members, the friends who knew you before Christ and want to question this whole God thing you're doing, and the angry, belligerent colleagues who know what buttons to push in order to make you want to tuck away your salvation. These things are our scorpions, our thorns, and our briers. These are the things that cause us pain, frustration, and anguish. We cannot hold back the love of Christ from them, as it can change them from who they were to who God purposed them to be. It is not our place to decide who stays in hell and who gets into heaven. You are only to speak the Word of God with the energy granted to you by Him.

If you read further in this text, you will learn that God is not speaking of natural food, but of the actual Word of God. God provides Ezekiel with a scroll that he ate, but God made the scroll taste like honey so that he might be equipped to go into Israel and speak the Word of God. Likewise, we cannot enter into the lives of those God has charged us to witness to malnourished and unfed. Get into the Word, grow in the Scriptures, and do not try to feed someone else off the regurgitated sermon you heard days, weeks, or months prior. Seek the face of the Father, learn for yourself, and eat for yourself so that you may speak to the thorns, briers, and scorpions without fear of their words or actions.

Mighty God, You are the source of my courage. You give me the strength I need to complete the tasks you've assigned. Thank You for reminding me through Your Word that you meet my needs and give me more than enough, even from unexpected places. In Jesus' name, I bow before You, humbly asking for forgiveness for the times when I didn't move. I seek the confidence and courage to share my faith boldly with those You have placed around me. Holy Spirit, rekindle a flame within me. In Jesus' name, I pray and give thanks. Amen.

Happy New Year!

"Blessed (happy, fortunate, prosperous, and enviable) is the man who walks and lives not in the counsel of the ungodly [following their advice, their plans and purposes], nor stands [submissive and inactive] in the path where sinners walk, nor sits down [to relax and rest] where the scornful [and the mockers] gather. But his delight and desire are in the law of the Lord, and on His law (the precepts, the instructions, the teachings of God) he habitually meditates (ponders and studies) by day and by night" (Ps 1:1-2 AMPC).

Each year we start with a new zeal, a new passion, a new thirst to achieve some goal. Lose weight. Save money. Make better decisions. And for some, spend more time in prayer and get involved in church. Well, all these things are great and can lead us to better lives. However, how often do we accomplish these goals successfully? We may run the race with fervor up until May or June, but by then things begin to fizzle out. Nevertheless, the achievement of your goals/resolutions, no matter how spiritual or natural, will be easier depending on the company you keep.

The text says that who you hang out with will determine how blessed, happy, and fortunate you will be. Therefore, I challenge you to assess your relationships. What type of people do you surround yourself with? Do you "hang" with co-workers who do not come in on time and who leave early? Are you surrounding yourself with and take advice from people not driven by the things of God? Are you dulling your passion and zeal for virtue and righteousness because you are "accepted" by a certain group of people? Or better yet, is hanging out with believers who fail to challenge your deeds, actions, and thoughts better than hanging out with those "holy rollers" who never seem to have fun?

Remember that each day is an opportunity for a fresh start, so even if you are reading these in the middle of the summer, choose to start fresh. Which will you choose? Will you delight in the Word of God, submitting your heart, body, and soul to Him so He can mold you into His image. Or will you accept the advice, guidance, and encouragement of those around you who have no more authority in this life than you? So, what will you choose…?

Heavenly Father, my Lord and my King, I come before You, humbly asking that You help us to weed out those who we may be comfortable with but who may not be the best for us. Help us to recognize and understand that we outgrow people as we mature and grow in You, but we never outgrow Your divine instruction. Your Word lives, and Your Spirit speaks to every situation. Daddy, guide us, strengthen us, and provide us with the ability to relinquish control in our lives. Help us to push aside our evil desires, push aside our good intentions, and cling to the words from Your mouth and the teachings of Your word. Give us a new fire, a new passion, and a new thirst for You that can't be quenched simply in Sunday service. Holy Spirit, remind us that You reign in our lives, that Your voice is always speaking, and that we simply have to sit still to hear it. In Jesus' name. Amen.

Being Made New

"Consequently, from now on we estimate and regard no one from a [purely] human point of view [in terms of natural standards of value]. [No] even though we once did estimate Christ from a human viewpoint and as a man, yet now [we have such knowledge of Him that] we know Him no longer [in terms of the flesh]. Therefore if any person is [ingrafted] in Christ (the Messiah) he is a new creation (a new creature altogether); the old [previous moral and spiritual condition] has passed away. Behold, the fresh and new has come!" (2 Cor 5:16-17 AMPC).

The text says that if a person is "ingrafted" in Christ, they are made new. When something is ingrafted, it is made a part of something, in such a way that there is *no* distinction between the old and new elements. Are you ingrafted or simply splicing together random elements? I am sure you're as puzzled as I was when the Holy Spirit challenged my heart with this blend of Scripture and biology. Ingrafted? Spliced? Well, let me define the two terms so that it makes a bit more sense:

Ingrafted: cause to grow together
parts from different plants
Spliced: the joining of two things
end-to-end to make new

When something is ingrafted, the new skin (muscle, bone, thought process, etc.) takes over the old, decaying the destructive part of you. However, when something is spliced together, the new elements are just connected to the end of the old, making things appear longer or larger, but there is no change. When we simply splice the Spirit of God to our old life—the life we're comfortable with; the life that is full of sin, frustration, anger, lies, etc.—we aren't doing anything to make sure our lives are a reflection of Christ.

So, ask yourself this: Can people see the old you or the workings and image of Christ? The indwelling of Christ should take over your old ways so that you become a full element of the Spirit that dwells within you. In medicine, grafting is a long, assiduous process. It is painful, it is ugly, and it takes a while for that full recovery to occur. Where are you in the grafting processes? Have you accepted that for you to be new in Christ you must endure the ugly, hurtful, long process to return to your original position? The original form that God intended for you will come with time—time seeking His face and walking in His presence. Do you need to cut out or cut away the feelings of lust, doubt, fear, jealousy, and depression, then graft in Christ? Graft in His love, graft in His purity, and graft in His forgiveness, His mercy, His view of you, His vision, and His purpose. Allow Him to take over your whole self. Put aside the elements that are holding you in a position of stagnation, which will prevent you from obtaining the power and authority that will truly allow you to do more in Him.

Great Physician, the one capable of healing me from the inside out, healing wounds that for so long I have simply covered without properly treating, thank You for making me new. Father, show me the areas that need to be changed. Give me the strength to endure the grafting process, deepen my faith in You, and fully trust in You. I fall before You humbly, desiring that You use me to draw others to You. Holy Spirit, keep the fire burning for the presence of God. In the name of Jesus, I pray. Amen.

Canceled Plans

"There is no [human] wisdom or understanding or counsel [that can prevail] against the Lord. The horse is prepared for the day of battle, but deliverance and victory are of the Lord" (Prv 21:30-31 AMPC).

In the months following my college graduation, I had everything planned out for the rest of my 20s (and 30s, if I am honest). I knew when I would get married (and to whom), how many children I would have (and when), and the next steps in my career (from classroom teacher to school counselor), only for God to reveal this Scripture as comfort as He canceled my plans. I am sure that many of you can relate to that feeling. Having a plan in mind helps in all sorts of ways, but those plans can also turn into an idol if we aren't careful. In society, financial and professional achievements are highly adored. No matter the setting, whether in a boardroom or a church, being in leadership and having a title are important. Unfortunately, we can let those goals overwhelm our minds, blocking out our thoughts of God. Early morning meetings replace devotional time, yard work becomes a Sunday morning chore instead of corporate worship, and we slowly find ourselves worshiping our calendar and to-do list above the Creator of all.

God reminded me through life's experiences and His word that no matter what I plan, what I think, or how much I try to prepare, God's purpose and plans will ALWAYS supersede what I think will happen. I also learned through this time to seek out God's direction and desires for my life, and I accepted that discipline is an important habit to maintain, sometimes daily. Sometimes you can rely on the most "recent" directions given; other times a daily update is necessary so that you do not move out of order.

The laid-out plans that I mentioned did not come to fruition; they only led to feelings of frustration, both with myself and with God. However, I can tell you that I did end up getting married (not the same guy), and having children (after years of fertility treatments), and I have yet to begin work as a school counselor, but if it is in God's plan, then it will come in His time. And while I wait (some days patiently; other days not so much), I still turn to God. Asking for His direction as I wait. Asking if there is another role He needs me to fulfill so that I may be His hands and feet on Earth. I'm learning to accept that His will and wisdom are greater than mine in so many ways.

Daddy, I praise You for Your Word. I thank You for constantly reminding me that my life is not my own. I am a vessel to be used by You to help others experience Your love and grace. Holy Spirit, continue to convict my heart so that I may grow in You, relying on Your promptings to keep me focused on God's guidance and not my own goals. Help me to continue to put aside my calendar and to-do list so that it may not become an idol, taking the place as the head of my life. In Jesus' name, I pray. Amen.

Courageous Change

"[Motivated] by faith he left Egypt behind him, being unawed and undismayed by the wrath of the king; for he never flinched but held staunchly to his purpose and endured steadfastly as one who gazed on Him Who is invisible" (Heb 11:27 AMPC).

I wonder if you have shared this same experience. When I first moved out on my own, I moved into my apartment alone. Before I had the chance to move in all my furniture, I spent a night in that apartment on an air mattress, jumpy at each sound, nervous about whether I had locked the doors and the windows even though I was on the third floor. It was a new experience and a new place, and it was a change that caused me to feel a little afraid.

This verse, however, shows a different response to change. The "he" in this passage is Moses, who sets a great example for how we should respond when God prompts us to make a move that can cause us to feel fear. We are to remain focused on the purpose that God has given each of us when He directs us to move. We cannot be overwhelmed by the heartache or the trouble that change will bring each of us, and change will bring "trouble." In my situation, my "trouble" was adjusting to being alone, doing things for myself that used to be my parents' responsibility, and creating a new level of accountability since I no longer had the "safety net" of a house full of people. Your troubles may be a change in financial stability if God prompts you to leave your full-time job to serve as a missionary, or it may be a shift in your family dynamics if God prompts you to adopt a child from another culture.

Both of these examples are excellent life changes, but they will result in troubles that you should face bravely.

We must remember that someone else has gone before us on this journey. God is the Alpha and Omega (Rv 1:8). He has seen our life from beginning to end. This should help us to remain on the path set before us. This should strengthen us to endure the negative comments, the feelings of separation that come with transitions, and the feelings of guilt and shame we feel for the choices we have made. You, with God's help, will remain committed to the plan and see it through to completion because you are not alone.

Daddy, I worship Your name. You are worthy to be praised and lifted up above all things on the earth. Thank You for continuing to mold me and build me up as my faith grows in You. Help me to remember that You are before me and always with me as I walk through the transitions You have purposed for me. I am not alone. You are there to comfort me and strengthen me. Your Word gives me wonderful examples of those You have assigned lives of transition and change, and I am no different. Just as You were with Moses, You are with me. As You were with Abraham, You are with me. As You were with Mary and Joseph, You are with me. And I thank You for Your loving kindness and protection. In Jesus' name, I pray. Amen.

Happy Feelings

*"Let us rejoice and shout for joy [exulting and triumphant]!
Let us celebrate and ascribe to Him glory and honor, for the
marriage of the Lamb [at last] has come, and His bride has
prepared herself" (Rv 19:7 AMPC).*

My husband and I have been married for ten years. This
year, in the days leading up to our anniversary, I took
to social media and posted a picture of us together. On one
particular day, I posted a series of pictures of us together at
different weddings. These pictures included weddings that
we both participated in and some we attended as guests.
And there was even one picture from before we even
started dating.

As I reflected each day on different moments in my marriage, I thought about the highs and lows of those ten years.
More importantly, I thought about the day of our wedding
ceremony. On her special day, a bride may have butterflies
and even chilly feet, but she knows that from that day forward, she's committing to make her groom happy. Will she
be perfect? No. Will she intend to hurt her groom? No. Likewise, on that day, the groom stands with similar thoughts
in mind. He wants to keep his bride happy, to make her feel
protected and secure, and to feel loved without a doubt.

The relationship between God and His bride (that's us,
guys!) is the same. It's one of love and joy. Now, if we are to
be the bride of Christ, we should desire to make God happy
through our thoughts and actions, and just like the groom
on his wedding day, God will be intentional in making sure

we each feel loved, protected, secure, and filled with an unexplainable joy. That should be an ever-present reminder of who we live to please. If all of heaven rejoiced when Christ joined Himself to each of us, then we should walk in the righteousness that He desires from each of us. Now, if we're really being honest, will we do things to hurt God? Absolutely! Will we do it on purpose? No. Well, if we are really being honest, then the answer may be yes. We may do things even though we know it will grieve the Spirit. Am I right?! However, that should not be our intention always; we should make it a priority to do things that will make the heart of God swell. You might ask, "Diayle, what things? I go to church, I serve in ministries, I give during offering time, etc." Well, ask yourself: What is your devotional time (prayer, worship, and scripture reading) like? Is it a to-do list item or a time that you look forward to with expectation and excitement? How about your relationships with others? Are you loving your neighbors as yourself (Lv 19:18) and serving "the orphans and widows" around you (Jas 1:27)? These are just two areas that require each of us to examine our schedules and our hearts.

God of Love, I praise your Holy name simply for who You are. You are love, a perfect example of unconditional love, and I am so glad that I get the chance to rest in that love. I apologize for the times when I choose to hurt You with my thoughts and actions. Will You forgive me? Holy Spirit, help me to choose You in the future above my desires. In Jesus' Name. Amen.

Who Do You Turn To?

"Then the mariners were afraid, and each man cried to his god; and they cast the goods that were in the ship into the sea to lighten it for them. But Jonah had gone down into the inner part of the ship and had lain down and was fast asleep. So the captain came and said to him, What do you mean, you sleeper? Arise, call upon your God! Perhaps your God will give a thought to us so that we shall not perish" (Jon 1:5-6 AMPC).

*** Read the chapter in its entirety ***

Oftentimes, when the book of Jonah is studied, the focus is on the actions and decisions of Jonah. But it is equally important to look at the behaviors of the sailors who were with him in the first chapter. Preachers have compared believers to Jonah during sermons, challenging us to think differently about running away from the things that God has called us to do, but there are times we behave like these sailors more than we behave like Jonah. When things started to get crazy on their ship, these *trained* sailors began to panic and turn to their gods, but that didn't change or end the chaos that they were experiencing. They even went as far as throwing away things of value to find relief from the storm. Unfortunately, you and I are guilty of the same thing. We turn to our "gods" (friends or family, drugs and alcohol, or inappropriate sexual relationships), hoping that anyone or anything will solve our problems…will calm our storms.

After trying their gods, they turned to Jonah, asking him to call on his God to save them. Like the sailors, we eventually do the same, turning to the God of Jonah after trying things our way. We must come to terms with the things we turn to before we turn to God, then skip that step, seeking God first to calm our storms. Once we identify what we turn to before we turn to God, we can prevent the need to sacrifice things of value (our time, money, personal and professional advancements, etc.). Turning to the Comforter, the Holy Spirit, to ease the pain and alleviate the fears and frustrations of life allows us to see what God is capable of. It reassures us of His faithfulness and power. The sailors learned the same lesson in verse sixteen of the same chapter.

I challenge you to think about the things that you have turned to in the past in order to comfort yourself during life's storms. I know that I've turned to a variety of things during times of frustration and sadness. Some were healthy choices, such as worship music, exercising, and prayer. Others weren't, like pornography. Making the godly choice each time we're faced with storms requires us to create new habits, which takes time. Give yourself grace as you identify your gods.

Heavenly Father, You are ever-present and so patient when I turn to other gods before You, and for that I thank You! Forgive me for the time that I have wasted seeking out comfort in other places rather than turning to You for direction and guidance. Thank You for Your grace and love while I go through life's storms. As I continue through life, help me to put aside the gods I once turned to so that I may learn to turn to You first. Entering Your presence in prayer and worship, knowing that in Your presence are wisdom, joy, and comfort, will allow me to endure the most difficult challenges. Thank You. Amen.

To Each Their Own

"To one he gave five talents [probably about $5,000], to another two, to another one—to each in proportion to his own personal ability. Then he departed and left the country" (Mt 25:15 AMPC).

I heard this verse during a 90-day Bible challenge that I participated in recently. Each participant was to read along while the Bible was read aloud, and then a discussion was held about the text for that specific day. On this particular day, this verse that I'd heard many times before resonated differently. Many of us are familiar with this parable. Three servants are given a job to complete while their master is away. One servant gets right to work and doubles what he'd been given. The second servant also doubles what he was given. The last servant is so scared that he buries the master's gold, because his master is sinister and he's afraid of the outcome. He gets reprimanded for his actions, but he was capable of doing what was asked of him. He received a bag because his PREVIOUS success proved he was able to earn his master's money.

My first thought that morning was that he failed, not because he was incapable, but because he was afraid of the pressure, of the responsibility, of being "put on the spot." He doubted himself and was nervous about meeting someone else's expectations. Many of us are so capable of being successful, but when given the opportunity, we flounder because we're afraid of rising to the occasion.

This servant was capable and had the ability to succeed, but fear caused his failure. Self-doubt led him to bury his chance to prove himself. He got in his own way, and his mindset limited his advancement. We have to do the same; we have to stop getting in our own way. We each have the ability to prove to our Master that we can follow through. Stop letting your identified abilities get buried in the dirt! There have been times when I have buried my talents in the dirt because I was afraid of rejection, afraid that people would think about me differently, all the time denying the ability that God fashioned within me. Have you also buried gifts and talents because of fear? Have you buried your abilities because you think you don't deserve them or because someone has told you that you don't deserve them because of your past? Remember, you've been given these talents, this task, this responsibility, not just because you have the ability, but because of your previous experience. You've already proven that you're capable. God has called you to more because you have proven that you can handle it.

Faithful Servant, You are an amazing example. You move with authority, strength, and courage. I have gifts and talents that I desire to use for Your glory, but there are times when I feel afraid, doubtful, and uncertain. Am I enough? Am I worthy? Will I get it right? In those times, I need Your help to walk courageously, righteously, and with the authority that You have given me. Thank You for choosing me to do Your work here on Earth. Thank You for recognizing the abilities even when I do not recognize them within myself. Amen.

Small but Mighty

"Behold, I will make you to be a new, sharp, threshing instrument which has teeth; you shall thresh the mountains and beat them small, and shall make the hills like chaff" (Is 41:15 AMPC).

In this chapter of Isaiah, God reminds us that He supports us at all times. But in Isaiah 41:15, in every version I have studied, it spoke about being made into a new tool: a strong, sharp threshing instrument that is able to crumble mountains. Exciting, right? But a threshing instrument is a tool intended to separate grain, not a demolition machine, so how can that be? With the power and backing of a great God, we'll each be made sharper and stronger than the mountains (insecurity, doubt, fear, negative self-talk, or rejection) before us.

There was a period in my life when I decided to try my hand at direct sales in order to earn extra money. If you aren't familiar, direct sales companies require their sales representatives to get customers to either purchase individual products or enroll in an auto-shipment program for products. This type of job was so out of the norm for me. I was used to engaging my students and following lesson plans with an expected outcome or goal. But with this position, I had no real plan. When I started this journey, I gave it my very best. I went to trainings (in-person and virtual), read books for development, and more. But the biggest thing I had to deal with to improve was internal. I had to handle my insecurity and fear of rejection. In a role like this one, rejection came often, but I still had to put on a brave face, and this passage helped me not only in the world of work but also in my faith walk. Even now, as I write this book filled with open, honest transparency, I must be brave, knowing that God has "backed" me.

This reassurance makes doing things scared a little easier. As we earnestly seek after God, after His perfect peace, joy, healing, and more, we'll get a bit stronger. Our discernment will become sharper, moments of prayer more powerful, and with each area of growth, mountains will crumble even more! You and I are instruments that God wants to use. Unfortunately, we get in our own way at times, thinking ourselves too small, insufficient, or insignificant, but God knows that if we rely on His power and might, we can be transformed into a mighty weapon.

The Lord who is my rock, my fortress, and my Savior, You are my strength when I am weak and afraid. There have been times when my fear has stopped me from being the person You have designed me to be, and for that I am sorry. Thank You for Your presence, which makes me better, which brings freedom, and which transforms me into the person You've crafted me to be. You created me for something, helped me to uncover that very thing, and, even more importantly, helped me to see my mountains, which, together, we need to demolish for Your glory and my good. In the name of Jesus. Amen.

Gut Check

"A time will come, however, indeed it is already here, when the true (genuine) worshipers will worship the Father in spirit and in truth (reality); for the Father is seeking just such people as these as His worshipers" (Jn 4:23 AMPC).

S ometimes we need to have a "gut check"! As we continue in our journey with Jesus, we become complacent; our times in prayer are limited to a quick fix in the morning or reading an e-votional as we check our email before getting out of bed in the morning. I know I've been in that place a time or two, especially when life seems like it's moving faster than I can keep up with. But in those moments, we have to ask ourselves this: Am I really worshiping the Father in spirit and in truth? Am I taking time out to check where I stand with Him? Are my actions internal, external, or eternal? Look inside yourself and see what your motives are. Are you simply doing this "God thing" in order to avoid hell, or have you genuinely come to serve Him? Have you come to take from the Father without giving anything in return?

At times we have to think of our relationship with God like a savings account. In order for an account to accrue interest, there must be an initial deposit, and you can liken that to your coming to God and giving your life over to Him. That's when interest begins, and every day more and more is added to that original amount, but you can't expect to truly grow your amount (especially not with the current interest rates, but that's a talk for another day) if you fail to make deposits into the account. Now, let's be clear. I'm not talking actual currency, but at times the return on our investment comes in an increase of peace, joy, patience, and more. When we spend that time praying more for others than asking for things for ourselves, we grow in faith as we see God work on behalf of others. Within our relationships, we must make deposits of time, energy, money, and emotions. Our relationship with God is no different. We can't expect God to constantly pour into us if we fail to put in the work ourselves. If we fail to make deposits, we won't experience an increase.

Together, during those times when our relationship with God seems mundane, we must take action. We must check our motives. We must check our progress, asking ourselves if we are moving forward or staying the same.

Heavenly Father, You are everything! You are constant, faithful, and gracious. You are gentle and loving, and I am so grateful for the love You continue to reveal through Your Word. You desire a worshiper who will shower You with the reverence and adoration that You deserve. At times I forget, and I'm sorry. But thank You for giving me another opportunity to get it right. I pray that I remember this gut check when I start to waver, that I may turn to You, making deposits in our relationship, giving You what You are due. In Jesus' name. Amen.

Allow Me to Introduce Myself

"Nor shall your name any longer be Abram [high, exalted father]; but your name shall be Abraham [father of a multitude], for I have made you the father of many nations" (Gn 17:5 AMPC).

I am a lover of words. I love to read. I love to look up the definitions of words I know (or think I know) and those that I don't. While this has been a plus for me academically and professionally as a teacher and counselor, it has caused trouble at times when communicating with others. If a word or phrase is used in a certain way, there have been times when I have hurt someone else or when I have been hurt by someone's words. Now, most times this happens unintentionally. A word or phrase has a particular meaning or intent to the speaker and is received differently by the hearer. This is true with names. Either legal names or nicknames. How we identify someone else can play a major part in how they interact with us and how they view themselves.

Throughout the Old and New Testaments, we witness God change the names of prominent leaders. In Genesis 17, we watch as Abram gets upgraded with a change in his name. He changed from "exalted father" to the "father of a multitude." This name change came with a promise: God was going to bless Abraham and his wife, Sarah (she also got a name upgrade), with a child since they had been unable to conceive and were beyond childbearing years. As time went on, Abraham tried achieving the desired outcome through his own means (yeah, I know it was Sarah's suggestion, but he went along with it) in order to experience God's promise.

Unfortunately, this choice led to the "faulty" execution of God's promise, a choice that led to bitterness, resentment, and anguish, and he still had to wait for God's promise to come to pass. But with a renewed commitment and a change of identity—how he saw himself and what others called him—Abraham was able to posture himself to walk into God's promises. So I'd like to ask you this: What are you calling yourself? After you've failed to make the best choices, what do you call yourself? When you move in your own time instead of waiting for God's timing, do you belittle yourself, or do you recognize that you aren't alone in making mistakes? After seeking forgiveness, do you call yourself "forgiven," or is "sinner" still your name? Can you see yourself as God sees you? Do you see yourself as loved? A chosen priest? Successful? Joyful?

In the times when making the right choices is difficult, when it seems almost impossible to avoid temptation, I encourage you to open God's Word to Genesis 18:14 and read this when you are unsure of who you are, when you doubt what God can do with your flaws and failures, or when things don't appear as they should. *"Is anything too hard or too wonderful for the Lord? At the appointed time, when the season [for her delivery] comes around, I will return to you and Sarah shall have borne a son. [Matt. 19:26]"* (Gn 18:14 AMPC)

I mentioned I love to look at the definition of words, so I would like to share three definitions of words found in Genesis 18:14, which I think are essential to remember in challenging times. Dictionary.com defines "hard" as "unyielding to pressure and impenetrable or almost impenetrable."[1] "Wonderful" is described as "excellent, great, marvelous."[2] You get the picture. These two adjectives are used to describe what God is capable of, and I'm sure we've heard this all

---

[1] *Dictionary.com, s.v.* "hard," accessed May 23, 2020,
http://dictionary.reference.com.

[2] *Dictionary.com,* s.v. "wonderful," accessed May 23, 2020,
http://dictionary.reference.com.

before, but sometimes we question His power and might. We question His definition of wonderful because, from our view, it doesn't look too good. But the last word I want to point out is "appointed." That word makes the entire verse more exciting to me. If something is appointed, it is "preset, pre-arranged, or set"[3] in the future to be regarded when making plans! God knows your life, as well as mine, beginning to end.

We each have an appointed time when He will come in and upgrade us, changing our names from sinner to beloved, changing our status from barren to mother (even if not to biological children). No matter what our lives look like at the moment, His power and might are more than enough to change it from hard to wonderful. But as He works, we must also acknowledge and respond to our new name, change what we call ourselves, and make sure others know that we've been made new. So please allow me to reintro-duce myself. They call me FORGIVEN. LOVED. ENOUGH. BEAUTIFUL. FAVORED. CHOSEN. EXECUTIVE. LEADER. LENDER. And so much more.

Mighty God, I thank You for being consistent, loyal, and loving despite all my flaws and imperfections. I am so thankful that You reveal new things in stories that I've read before, and You continue to provide understanding and insight through Your Word so that I may be made into your likeness more and more each day. Help me to see You within these pages so that I may learn more of Your char-acter and internalize it as I walk in that likeness. In Jesus' name, I pray for a change in mindset so that I may see myself as what I am becoming rather than what I was. Amen.

---

[3] *Dictionary.com*, s.v. "appointed," accessed May 23, 2020, http://dictionary.reference.com.

Action

A behavior, when executed fully, that is pivotal in the process of completing something with the purpose of achieving an expected and/or desired outcome. This process requires intentionality, changes in behavior, and the follow through in areas of challenge.

"Whatever may be your task, work at it heartily (from the soul), as [something done] for the Lord and not for men, Knowing [with all certainty] that it is from the Lord [and not from men] that you will receive the inheritance which is your [real] reward. [The One Whom] you are actually serving [is] the Lord Christ (the Messiah)" (Col 3:23-24 AMPC).

Are You Ready for War?

"Proclaim this among the nations: Prepare war! Stir up the mighty men! Let all the men of war draw near, let them come up. Beat your plowshares into swords, and your pruning hooks into spears; let the weak say, I am strong [a warrior]! Hasten and come, all you nations round about, and assemble yourselves; there You, O Lord, will bring down Your mighty ones (Your warriors)" (Jl 3:9-11 AMPC).

For ten years, I worked as a high school Social Studies teacher. I taught a range of subjects, but the one I loved the most was United States History. So when I first came across this passage, it struck a chord with me naturally as I reflected on the changes countries have made throughout history in preparation for war. I read these verses in several translations. Each time, I viewed it through the lens of spiritual warfare, even though the verses refer to preparing for an actual battle. I saw the reminder that everyone must be ready and equipped for the spiritual battle we must fight daily, but that requires a change in our thinking, our tools, and our tactics.

In verse nine, all nations were told to get ready for war; this requires a change in the people's mindset (thinking). In the United States, during World War II, the nation had to change in order to prepare and support the war. They had to think about what they could do as individuals to help the nation get ready. They had to figure out what they could sacrifice, what changes could be made, and so on. Verse ten requires us to change our tools, turning plowshares into swords. In the 1940s, car manufacturers stopped making cars and instead made tanks, changing the tools they produced so the nation could be equipped. Lastly, verse eleven is the call to action, the implementation of our tactic. "Come quickly! Get a move on! We're ready to fight!" Believers must war together at times, joining together in worship, fasting for the benefit of others, and being open to sharing struggles so that others may pray along with them.

I ask you this, then: Are you changing your thinking to change your tools? Are you thinking that your God is greater, stronger, or higher than everything, or do your problems seem insurmountable? Which mindset do you have when going into the spiritual battle for your life, family, health, and the world? Is it a mindset of power or defeat? If you are unsure, you should change your tools. Your prayers should shift from passive (weak) prayers—"If you would like, God"—to aggressive, big, and bold prayers (warrior-like)— "God, I know with everything in me that You can change things, and I have the authority to ask You to flip everything upside down." Have you brought your tools (prayer, fasting, and worship) to the battlefield, along with the right tactics, joining the fight with others, or are you keeping yourself closed off and limited?

Jehovah Nissi, the Lord Our Banner (victory), You go before me as I fight against the thief whom Christ warns of in John 10:10. In Your presence, I experience joy, strength, and peace, but I must guard against what may come. Father, forgive me for times when I have been afraid to come to You boldly with strength and assurance so that You can do great things in my life and the lives of those around me. I am trusting and believing in a miraculous change. For complete healing of physical bodies, hearts, and minds. I am believing in the restoration and reconciliation of relationships, for an outpouring of Your Spirit across the nation, and for Your children to be the change agents that You have created them to be. Help me today to walk in greater authority than I did yesterday, In Jesus' name. Amen.

A Longing Touch

"For she kept saying, If I only touch His garments, I shall be restored to health" (Mk 5:28 AMPC).

Recently, I have been reading the New Testament, specifically the books of Mark and Romans, and certain things have jumped out to me, challenging me to focus on pursuing God rather than waiting on God to answer my questions, grant my "wishes," and fulfill my requests at the drop of a hat. This verse from Mark is a "soundbite" taken from the story of the Woman with the Issue of Blood, and it challenged me to keep pushing to get closer to Him.

This woman was so determined, focused, and passionate. She did not seek answers. She didn't seek direction. She didn't seek guidance or wisdom. She simply sought Him. She passionately pursued Him, desiring to be in His presence, not just on the outskirts of the crowd, but up close and personal. That's the mindset we need to have at all times: during times of worship, when listening to the preached word, and during quiet reflection and study. We have to seek after Him. We have to fight through the crowds (distraction, feelings of disconnect, doubt, fear, self-condemnation, and a lack of clarity and understanding) to get to Him, to be so close that we can touch Him.

Do you know what challenged me the most? Her position! She was so low, in a position that would have put her on her face, on the ground, crawling, without the ability to see those around her, avoiding the crazy, confused looks of those she pushed past to touch the hem (the edge or border of a garment, especially at the bottom) of His garment. This is a position that society has taught us to avoid. We do not want to get low. We do not want to humble ourselves to hear from God. We want to be in a position of entitlement. We use the authority we have as an argument for why we make demands from God. Yes, He tells us that we can come boldly to His throne in order to seek out His wisdom, to ask for things, and to take on His rest and peace. Unfortunately, we do not always come with a sincere heart. A heart focused on being made anew. A heart focused on changing our character through redemption and repentance. A heart not focused on getting things, being "blessed" with materials, or receiving all that we have ever wanted. Jesus does not equal genie!

We must get low, fighting in the dirt, covered with dust, to feel the intimacy that will result in the change we desire! Being facedown needs to be our new position of worship.

Jesus, You are the wonderful counselor, our Mighty God, and the healer of my broken places, and I thank You for Your continued love and protection. Thank You for noticing and healing my needs, even when I feel unnoticed. I praise You and thank You for continuing to teach me through Your Word. Thank You for reminding me that even in the lowest position, covered with dirt and underfoot, You can bless me. Change my heart from feeling entitled when entering Your presence to feeling grateful and appreciative. In Jesus' name. Amen.

Dinner Guest

"And Levi (Matthew) made a great banquet for Him in his own house, and there was a large company of tax collectors and others who were reclining [at the table] with them. Now the Pharisees and their scribes were grumbling against Jesus' disciples, saying, Why are you eating and drinking with tax collectors and [preeminently] sinful people? And Jesus replied to them, It is not those who are healthy who need a physician, but those who are sick. I have not come to arouse and invite and call the righteous, but the erring ones (those not free from sin) to repentance [to change their minds for the better and heartily to amend their ways, with abhorrence of their past sins]" (Lk 5:29-32).

Also see Matthew 9:10-13 and Mark 2:16-19

I was attending a small group session recently, and we were discussing the story in the passages above. We see Jesus attending a dinner party hosted by Matthew and "eavesdrop" on a conversation that Jesus is having with the Pharisees, who are questioning why Jesus would attend a dinner and knowingly surround Himself with "wicked sinners." However, something that appeared consistently with each recount of this story is that the Pharisees were also there. The very people who thought less of all the invited guests were at the dinner! My mind began to wonder. Had they been invited (probably not)? Did they eat food prepared by these "low-life" people (probably)? Were they confronted by Christ for being judgmental (definitely)?

Outside of the common comparison that says many people in today's churches are like these Pharisees, I began to think those dudes were crazy! These "accusers," people who looked down on those whom Christ identified as being sick and needing His cure, failed to recognize that they were at the dinner, too. They were in a position to also receive the cure but were so far gone in their **self-righteousness** illness that they couldn't even appreciate what God arranged for them. How often do we do the same? Arriving at church with a grudge, entering into worship thinking it could sound better, or even skipping church altogether because a particular person isn't there. Unfortunately, we miss that, on that very day, a very special "meal" was prepared for us, and our healing cure was available. But we were too full of ourselves. Yet, if we were honest with ourselves, we would recognize our insanity. We do the same thing, day after day, week after week, year after year, not changing our behavior, but expecting a deeper level of intimacy with God. How about we go before the throne of grace with an open heart, ready to be changed, and begin praying for ourselves to change instead of praying for the "wicked" people in our lives to change, asking God to make us receptive of the change that is necessary to heal us and transform us.

Daddy, thank You for sending Your Son, Jesus, to heal my heart. Thank You for inviting me to the party, where I can receive Your healing touch, Your comforting Spirit, and Your sweet salvation. Today, help me to look deeper so I can draw closer to You, uncovering and healing places that I did not know needed a touch from you. In Jesus' name. Amen.

Doing It Scared

"Now faith is the assurance (the confirmation, the title deed) of the things [we] hope for, being the proof of things [we] do not see and the conviction of their reality [faith perceiving as real fact what is not revealed to the senses]" (Heb 11:1 AMPC).

If you are on social media, you may be familiar with the frequent use of "hashtags." A simple sign that used to be the pound sign on a telephone has taken on a new role. There was a time when the hashtag #doitscared was making its rounds on various social media platforms, mainly linked to professional risks, such as starting a new business or changing jobs. However, I took that as a challenge to my faith. This rational believer who came to Christ as a senior in high school, with no previous experience, who is Type A, who wants to know everything, was challenged to do her faith scared! I heard a pastor say once that a believer needs imagination to have faith, and at the moment I understood it, but after thinking more about it and reading over our verse for today, it took on a whole new meaning.

At the time, I was in a unique season. My children were preparing to start school for the first time outside of the home. I was debating if I was going to return to work and if I would return to a previous career or find a new one. I needed to use my imagination in that season, not my planner. Using my imagination sounded simple enough. I was surrounded by preschoolers then, each day prompting me to engage in pretend play and to create fairy tales. I realized "dreaming" up fairy tale perfection was easy, but you know what? So was dreaming up monsters in the closet and under the bed. In the same way, so is believing that your prayers are hitting the ceiling rather than being heard by God, as we see ourselves as being insufficient and unworthy. There have been periods when I have felt overwhelmed by things that I have been unable to plan for, but not this time!

From that moment on, I was intentional about allowing my imagination to fuel my faith. I will "dream" up a life filled with the joy, peace, loving grace of God, a family living a life of God's best, and so much more. Will you imagine along with me? What type of life do you see yourself having if you allow your imagination to run wild? Think of the things in Philippians 4:8. "Imagine" a John 10:10 life rather than constructing a "nightmare" of God not being who sixty-six books filled with 783,137 words (if we're counting in the King James Version) and countless testimonies tell us He is. Let's do it scared!

The Creator of heaven and Earth, the one who fashioned all things from Your imagination, thank You for creating me in Your image. Thank You for giving me the same creative ability. I am Your child. Help me to have the faith and imagination of a child, creating and dreaming of the greatness that You have promised me. A life of more. A life of abundance. Of peace, joy, and love. Forgive me for the times when my fears have limited what I know You can do in my life. I am sorry that I was shortsighted and unbelieving at times. Holy Spirit, help me to put aside any anxiety or fear that may limit me from seeing myself as You see me so that I may walk in freedom and faith and take the next steps forward in my life with You. In Jesus' name. Amen.

Salvation Requires Change

"For the grace of God (His unmerited favor and blessing) has come forward (appeared) for the deliverance from sin and the eternal salvation for all mankind. It has trained us to reject and renounce all ungodliness (irreligion) and worldly (passionate) desires, to live discreet (temperate, self-controlled), upright, devout (spiritually whole) lives in this present world, Awaiting and looking for the [fulfillment, the realization of our] blessed hope, even the glorious appearing of our great God and Savior Christ Jesus (the Messiah, the Anointed One), Who gave Himself on our behalf that He might redeem us (purchase our freedom) from all iniquity and purify for Himself a people [to be peculiarly His own, people who are] eager and enthusiastic about [living a life that is good and filled with] beneficial deeds" (Ti 2:11-14 AMPC).

John 3:16 tells us of God's great love for us. A love that was demonstrated not by sending flowers, buying candy, or even creating a mixtape (or YouTube playlist) of your favorite love songs. Instead, God showered us with love through the sacrifice of His Son, Jesus, but He did not stop there. God gave us His Spirit so that we might be delivered from that which keeps us bound, opening the "door" for us to draw closer to Him. Through growth and maturity, we learn to hate the things that go against the Father. We detest the things of the world.

But, to be honest, that can be hard! We are going to get it wrong. For some of us, we know how to act on the outside while the inner self remains unchanged. We should constantly strive for the greatness of Him, constantly moving toward His perfection, but we should also give ourselves the grace to know that we won't be perfect all the time and accept that each day is another chance to get better. That desire should grow steadily because He has already done so much for us. He gave His life so that we may be free from sin, free from punishment, free from hell, and free from bondage if we meditate on the things that His Spirit reveals to us through His Word and prayer. We should seek after Him as a perfect example of holiness and show our love for Him the same way He revealed it to us, through the sacrifice of our worldly desires.

Daddy, I am so thankful for the sacrifice of Your Son, Jesus. Thank You for caring enough about me even before I was born, or my parents were born, to send Your Son to redeem me. I thank You for Your Holy Spirit, which dwells within me, helping me to grow closer to You and love on You the way You deserve. Today, I honor You simply for who You are, and I appreciate all that You have already done in my life. Amen.

Moving with God

"At the Lord's command the Israelites journeyed, and at [His] command they encamped. As long as the cloud rested upon the tabernacle they remained encamped" (Nm 9:18 AMPC).

During their travels, the Israelites only moved when God moved. When His presence remained still, they encamped at that spot. We are to do the same. We cannot move before God says to move. Unfortunately, that is often our M.O. (method of operation). Real and imaginary deadlines, both professional and personal, drive our lives, pushing us to cut short the "wait time" necessary to find out where God would like us to go next. This can be hard to avoid. Between biological clocks, professional advancement deadlines, and frequent updates on social media, we are overwhelmed daily by others progressing in their lives, and we can be caught up in the moment.

Let's start by using the Israelites as our guide. Remember everything is in God's timing, however fast or slow that might seem to you or others. Remaining in place when God stops, using that time to seek out His guidance and direction, is so important, but we must be sensitive to His voice and aware of His presence. We do not have the luxury of a "cloud" revealing His presence or leading us on our journey, hovering over the places we should stop or moving forward for us to follow. Nevertheless, that does not mean we are unable to follow His lead. Sit still so that you may hear from Him. Do not allow too much to take over your life, preventing you from seeing or hearing Him move forward or stop so you will "encamp" where you are.

The Israelites allowed the cloud of God to lead them as they traveled, but they did not get it right, even though they had His presence with them. Understand that you may not always get it right, either. There may be times when you move too fast or sit too long, and you might miss the chance, but you have not been left to navigate the journey alone. "Let be and be still, and know (recognize and understand) that I am God. I will be exalted among the nations! I will be exalted in the earth!" (Ps 46:10 AMPC). Allow this verse to comfort you when you feel you've gotten out of step with the directions you have. Sit still where you are in prayer, in worship, and in mediation, thinking on God's Word and trusting that God always fulfills His promises (Is 55:11).

Heavenly Father, I praise You for Your continued guidance and direction, for constantly going before me, desiring to lead me toward a life of abundance. I pray for sensitivity to Your voice so that I may remain still when You call for it and advance when You lead me. Guard my heart and mind against the temptation to rush and the trap of comparison. You have written a just plan for each of Your children. Help me to walk in that plan and remain focused on the journey You have created before the foundation of the world. In Jesus' name, I pray. Amen.

Mountain High, Valley Low

"Then Jezebel sent a messenger to Elijah, saying, So let the gods do to me, and more also, if I make not your life as the life of one of them by this time tomorrow. Then he was afraid and arose and went for his life and came to Beersheba and Judah [over eighty miles, and out of Jezebel's realm] and left his servant there" (1 Kgs 19:2-3 AMPC).

In our walks with Christ, we'll have our ups and downs. However, it's essential to remember that God is in control. If we flip back a chapter, we find Elijah making "fools" of the Baal prophets, as well as praying for the return of the rain after a God-ordained drought. The miraculous works of Elijah prompted Israel to return to their true God, but it also caused Elijah's life to be threatened by the very woman who caused the people of Israel to sin against God in the first place. In a matter of moments, Elijah goes from an exuberant high to running for his life. Likewise, as believers, I'm sure you and I have gone from wonderful times of worship and prayer to seemingly running for our lives. There may not be a "hit" out on our lives, but life may just seem so overwhelming that we begin to run *from* our life rather than *for* our life.

I grew up in an interesting household. Although it seemed like other homes in the neighborhood from the outside—me, two working parents, my sibling, and, on occasion, even a dog—it was not totally what it seemed on the inside. I had a parent who dealt with substance abuse, which had an impact on my daily life throughout my childhood and even in my adulthood. If you share in that experience, you know there are high moments when living with someone struggling with addiction, but there can also be very low moments. I had my share of those times. Like a roller coaster, it was thrilling but also frightening. Unfortunately, that roller coaster ride did not just leave me with a funny feeling in my stomach; at times it made me want to run away from the life I knew. I found comfort, however, when I surrendered my life to Christ, when I had someone by my side as I endured the ups and downs of life.

In I Kings 19:5-9, God reveals His power and might by providing Elijah with three things: His presence, food for his weary body, and guidance so that he could continue to walk in the purpose God created him for. The God who is the same from the time of the Old Testament to today will do the same for you. Seek after Him. We cannot run for our lives, or from it, as a child of the King. Rather than running from the thing that threatens to take your very life, run into His arms and trust in His power.

During times when you feel like running, I pray that you intentionally seek out His presence, maybe through prayer or by singing along to your favorite worship playlist. I also pray that you take care of your physical body, choosing to feed yourself with healthy choices, not eating your emotions. I know for some of us, stress eating (for me it's ice cream and French fries; what is it for you?) and the results of those food choices can be more stressful than what caused the stress in the first place. Am I right?!? Lastly, I pray that you seek out His guidance moving forward. You can do this through prayer, fasting, and, depending on the situation, making adjustments around you. At times life can be so overwhelming, but when we learn to seek rest in the presence of God, practice self-care, and receive guidance for our next steps, we can enjoy the life that God has designed for us rather than trying to avoid it.

Daddy, You are a God of excellence, of love, of authority, and of power. I am so thankful that I can call on You when nothing else seems to be going right. I ask for a clear mind to hear from You and an open heart to learn from You. Help me to recognize areas of weakness so that I may be replenished in Your presence. Lead me and guide me as I continue to walk in Your ways above my own. In the name of Jesus, I pray. Amen.

Be Ready for the Rematch

"Then a prophet came to Ahab king of Israel and said, Thus says the Lord: Have you seen all this great multitude? Behold, I will deliver it into your hand today, and you shall know and realize that I am the Lord" (1 Kgs 20:13 AMPC).

"The prophet came to the king of Israel and said to him, Go, fortify yourself and become strong and give attention to what you must do, for at the first of next year the king of Syria will return against you" (1 Kgs 20:22 AMPC).

Temptations will always appear, but how we handle them shows our growth in our walks with the Father. Some will enter our lives as a small, simple temptation, something we think we can defeat and suppress without support of the Holy Spirit, like having an extra cookie for dessert. Other temptations are harder to battle, like the battle of addiction. But, as always, God reveals His desire for our lives through His Word and provides ways in which He can equip us to be better than before. In this chapter, Ahab is given the task of defeating the army set out to attack him, but he knew he'd be victorious. God gave him the strength and resources necessary to complete the task, as well as the reassurance of victory. Ahab and the young soldiers that God sent with him were successful in the defeat of the army. But in verse twenty-two, God tells Ahab that even after the defeat of the army, he had to return and strengthen himself and his army because he would return the following spring to face that same army again.

Friend, you and I both have to learn from this example. We will be tried and tested. We will face frustration, worry, and anxiety, but God will give us the resources we need to be successful and overcome the "army" coming against us. But remember that it will return...only stronger. We are each tempted by different things. Some struggle with pornography or other sexual sins. Others are overeating or overspending. So you cannot let up after the victory. You must return to your quiet time. You must maintain and increase your prayer life. You cannot gain strength without first breaking yourself down. You must sacrifice to hear from God. You have to open yourself up to be made whole and strong so you can move forward in the next battle. The "sacrifice" can look as spiritual (fasting from food, incorporating bible reading plans, or avoiding secular music) or as natural as you'd like (you don't have to answer that late night text or scroll through social media on the company time), but you'll have to "give to get." Just as Ahab and his army were charged with preparing for the first battle and remaining ready for battles in the future, you and I both need to remain in a posture and position of preparation so that we may battle temptation with strength, support, and God's backing.

Good, good Father, You are so worthy of praise, even though I are not always worthy to give it. I honor You and adore You for simply being God, not for anything that You have given me, but simply for who You are. Help me to listen to your promptings so that I may not fall into temptation. Help me use your Word to battle what's to come. In Jesus' name. Amen.

The Truth Will Set You Free

"So Jesus said to those Jews who had believed in Him, If you abide in My word [hold fast to My teachings and live in accordance with them], you are truly My disciples. And you will know the Truth, and the Truth will set you free" (Jn 8:31-32 AMPC).

Throughout life, we will strive to accomplish a number of things, but each item on our lifelong bucket list requires us to take an initial step, to have some starting point. Depending on what you want to accomplish (losing weight, saving money, or traveling the world), action is required, much like walking out your faith with Christ. In this passage, Jesus is teaching the Jews the importance of following His teachings. The part I found interesting is that this group of people is already familiar with the practices and traditions of God as found in the Jewish religion, but Jesus spoke out against many of their common practices. He especially spoke out against doing things out of obligation and requirement; rather, He spoke on the need for the application of His teachings.

Here, however, Jesus teaches them to take hold of His teachings. To hold onto something means to "grasp, grip, or clench." Or, as Jesus teaches here, we are to internalize what we gain from our intimate times with Him. We must take time to memorize Scripture, not to impress others, but to deepen our relationship with the only person who truly completes us. The text goes on to say we must "live in accordance with them," so we can't simply know what we are to do and where we should go, but we must apply it, make some external display of what we have made internal as we walk out this life that will lead to a blessed eternity.

A popular cliché is found in verse thirty-two. "The truth shall set you free." We've all heard it before, but it often relates to exposing a lie. The "truth" that Jesus speaks of is the Father, the one who can grant you a new life. A life free from depression, sexual sin, and thoughts of suicide. But you must first "abide" in the Word of God and apply it to your life. You cannot complain to God about remaining stuck in various sins if you haven't changed your life to reflect Him.

So, today, I encourage you to make a conscious decision to take action, to make a positive, progressive change that will set you free from an area that you feel stuck in. Be honest, seek God for help in that area, and ask for discernment on partnering with a professional, if necessary. I know it will be tough, but the reward requires refinement.

Daddy, I exalt You for another day. You are a God of excellence, a God of change, and a God of purpose. Thank You for continuing to call me into Your presence. I cannot thank You enough for surrounding me with Your presence, for reassuring me in times of complacency that I can still enter Your presence with confidence. Holy Spirit, help to remove distractions so that I may become more sensitive to Your voice. In Jesus' name, I pray. Amen.

Jumpstart

"After she had said this, she went back and called her sister Mary, privately whispering to her, The Teacher is close at hand and is asking for you. When she heard this, she sprang up quickly and went to Him" (Jn 11:28-29 AMPC).

We drop into the middle of a story with this passage. Mary was in a time of mourning. Lazarus, her brother, had been dead for four days. However, when she heard that Jesus was looking for her, she "sprang up quickly." She moved without hesitation or thought. I can only imagine the scene. She's crying, reflecting on times with her brother, accepting the consoling words of the surrounding crowd. But when she heard that Jesus desired her presence, she jumped up, probably startling her comforters, and ran to Christ.

I wonder... Are we responding the same way when God calls to us? Do we leap up wherever we are, throwing aside the people around us? Do we dismiss the thoughts that we were having so we can answer the call of God? In this passage, Jesus was simply calling Mary over to His location, but we have each had times in our lives when God has called us to some action: a call to ministry; a call to pray for, forgive, or comfort a person; or a call to share our testimony and witness to a crowd of unbelievers. But we fail to move! We fail to lift ourselves up to a position where we can fully be used. I wonder why. Is it because we don't feel like it, or are we waiting for confirmation from two, three, or eight people even though we know what God is telling us? Whatever it is, it is disobedience. If you didn't know before now, delayed obedience is, in fact, disobedience. When you and I fail to move when called, we have sinned against the Father. Everything has an appointed time, and if you don't move then, it will get done, just not by you. You may be thinking, "But it's still getting done, so why should I have to rush?" Well, the same can be said of Christ's assignment. Did He need to rush? Could someone else have completed His assignment if He failed to listen?

Think how often we rush. We rush around town on Black Friday. We rush in traffic. But oftentimes we fail to move when the lover of our souls—the King of kings, the Lord of lords, the one true God—calls us. There have been times when I've stubbed my toe while rushing to find my ringing cellphone, but I know there have been times when I haven't moved with this same urgency to respond to the voice of the Father.

So I think we need to ask ourselves this: Are there times when we're being unresponsive? Are there times when we're not in the right position to hear God's call at all.

Abba Father, we praise You, exalt You, and lift Your name on high. We cannot thank You enough for all the great things You have done in our lives. But we come to You humbly, petitioning You to open our eyes so we can see where we fail in You. Show us areas of weakness so that we may walk in the will and purpose that You destined us for, even before You created the stars in the sky. Make clear to us Your voice. Help us to be sensitive to Your command. Reveal to us areas of sin—not the blatant sins that we have learned to avoid daily, but the sins that so easily entangle us. The sins of omission. Holy Spirit, convict and correct. We have to endure the correction, the rebuke, and the "punishment" so that we may learn and mature in You. We lay our lives before You, returning to You what is rightfully Yours so that we may live lives that are pleasing to You, not our flesh. In Jesus' name, we pray and give thanks with a heart of gratitude. Amen.

Facing Your Fears

"But Jesus said to them, It is I; be not afraid! [I AM; stop being frightened!] Then they were quite willing and glad for Him to come into the boat. And now the boat went at once to the land they had steered toward. [And immediately they reached the shore toward which they had been slowly making their way.]" (Jn 6:20-21 AMPC).

There was a time when I tried my hand at blogging. I started pretty well. I posted regularly and engaged in conversations in the comments sections. The whole thing. Unfortunately, I started to fall off. Life started to get busy, so posts were published further and further apart, and the content became shorter and shorter. Until one day, when God challenged me to share a very private and personal story. He told me to tell the entire world—it is the internet, after all—that I was unable to conceive children. As you can imagine, I was not quick to post a blog about something that I saw as a major flaw in my body, my life, and my marriage. I failed to move on this command for several months. It was so private, so personal, and I couldn't possibly share it with everyone in the world. Not only would it reveal an area of hurt and embarrassment, but it would also reveal a major flaw in my personality: I, a control freak, was unable to control a particular area in my life.

As I continued to avoid God's direction, this passage challenged me. I was so convicted by this "in your face" command to live life without fear, and at the same time, I was being reminded that God's presence alone should comfort me. And His Word and promises should reassure me. As He walks along with me, in His timing, I should find comfort in the fact that "smooth sailing" will come. If we zoom out a few verses from this passage, we find the disciples battling strong winds, but Jesus joins them, simply by walking, after they've rowed for miles. He did not run or stress; He moved at His pace, and His presence was necessary for them to move forward faster and with ease. The Holy Spirit asked me this at that moment: Are you handing over the oars to let the Lord lead, or are you battling against Him as He tries to calm the seas? I want to challenge you with that same question: Are you willing to surrender your feelings of control to make the journey easier? Are you willing to let go of the thing that you are holding on to for "safety" so you can experience peace when surrounded by a storm?

Now, I will tell you, after this tough heart-to-heart with my Heavenly Father, I sat down at my computer and typed that blog post. I was transparent and open. I admitted to being a control freak and shared that I struggle with the effects of a disorder known as PCOS (Polycystic Ovary Syndrome), which was the cause of my fertility challenges. That post went live on my blog in May of that year. In June of that same year, my husband and I learned that we were pregnant with our first child. She was born the following February, and we learned that we were pregnant, without the aid of fertility treatment, with our second child that very same year. Throughout His Word, God continued to reveal to me that He is faithful, but also, even when what He asks can create a feeling of fear, it will work out for His glory and our good!

Jehovah Jireh, the Lord who will provide, thank You for each moment that You have provided for me. There are times in my life when You have provided resources, protection, wisdom, and guidance. Help me to put down my need to be in charge, the need to be in total control of the world around me, so that I may take hold of the peace, freedom, and joy that comes from relying on Your presence over my strength. In Jesus' name, I pray. Amen.

Getting Dressed

"Put on God's whole armor [the armor of a heavy-armed soldier which God supplies], that you may be able successfully to stand up against [all] the strategies and the deceits of the devil" (Eph 6:11 AMPC).

Read Ephesians 6:10-18 for more context

Recently, my husband and I celebrated our tenth wedding anniversary. We called it our "I Do Redo." We wanted to come together with friends and family and celebrate our big day all over again, because on our actual wedding day, a tornado came through the area that our ceremony and reception were held at, causing major damage and power outages. It made for a memorable evening, including dancing to the sounds of guests singing and using the decorations as lighting since there was no power at the venue. During our "I Do Redo," we played a game where guests had to guess whether the correct answer to a statement was my husband or me. One statement was, "I take longer to get ready." Many of our guests were correct in guessing my husband. Between getting the kids ready, completing last-minute things around the house, and trying to sleep in as long as possible, I have mastered the art of getting ready in about fifteen to twenty minutes tops!

Now, while that is great for mornings before work, when reflecting on this skill after our celebration, the Holy Spirit reminded me of this verse. He didn't limit the reminder to putting on clothes; He also extended it to how I saw my marriage and role as a mother. The night of the celebration, our family and friends shared words of encouragement and praise for what they've witnessed in our marriage. It felt great, but when I thought about it later, I wondered if we could live up to it. Again, the Holy Spirit reminded me of this verse. It's not just about the clothes. He explained that I am not ill-equipped to fight the various battles that I'll face in life, but I haven't always taken the time to get properly dressed.

God has supplied each of us with the same "armor," but we are not always using it. Can I ask you something? When was the last time you had on the "breastplate of righteousness" when faced with temptation? When was the last time you made sure the "helmet of salvation" was in place before leaving for work? Were the "shield of faith" and the "sword of the Spirit" with you at all times? Have you covered your feet with the "gospel of peace" when spending time with family?

While these are figurative elements of our spiritual wardrobe, they should not be forgotten. We cannot go out into a world in yoga pants, hoping for the best just for the sake of time; we have to enter into all circumstances fully equipped and ready. So, what should we be doing to make sure we're ready for all life has to throw at us? We should take the time each day to pray, read Scripture, and sing (off key, if necessary) songs of praise and worship. Allow God's Word to penetrate your mind throughout the day. Many Bible apps now feature various translations that will read aloud, so while getting ready for the day, listen to the Word of God and meditate on it before anything else can cloud your thoughts and mind. What other ways can you "get dressed" before fully engaging in your day?

God, as I continue on this journey of truth, power, and deeper intimacy, help me to see myself as You see me: strong, righteous, healed, and capable. I desire to know You more, no longer on my terms, but as You have designed, with You being Lord of my life, not my calendar or expectations. Help me to put aside my limited view of what I am up against, and reveal my areas of weakness so that I may be equipped for more. In Jesus' name. Amen.

Notes

CPSIA information can be obtained
at www.ICGtesting.com
Printed in the USA
FSHW020816091020
74544FS

9 781612 449029